# A BRIEF HISTORY OF THE CONSTITUTION AND GOVERNMENT OF MASSACHUSETTS

WITH A CHAPTER ON LEGISLATIVE PROCEDURE

BY

LOUIS ADAMS FROTHINGHAM, LL. B.

SPEAKER, MASSACHUSETTS HOUSE OF REPRESENTATIVES, 1904–1905
LIEUTENANT-GOVERNOR OF MASSACHUSETTS, 1908–1910
LECTURER AT HARVARD UNIVERSITY ON STATE AND
CITY GOVERNMENT IN MASSACHUSETTS

CAMBRIDGE
PUBLISHED BY HARVARD UNIVERSITY
1916

# PREFACE

This small volume is the outgrowth of a series of lectures given at Harvard University. It is put forth primarily for the use of students there, but it may also prove of assistance to the members of the General Court, to those who are interested in constitutional and historical matters, and at the present time, when a constitutional convention is contemplated, to those who may serve as delegates.

A book recently issued by the Commission on Economy and Efficiency entitled *Functions, Organization, and Administration of State Government*, covers the duties of the State officers and the Boards and Commissions, so I have omitted any detailed description of the powers and functions of those officials and bodies.

I wish to express my appreciation of the kindness of Professor Edward Channing who was good enough to read the chapters on the early history. To the efficient Clerk of the House of Representatives, Mr. James W. Kimball, who read the chapter on Legislative Procedure, I owe thanks for valuable suggestions. To Professor W. B. Munro, who advised publication and revised the material, I owe the encouragement to begin as well as to complete the work.

The author is conscious of many omissions and shortcomings in this book, but has endeavored to include in it data that seemed of most importance to those interested in study or casual investigation of constitutional and legislative matters. His apology for publication, if any be needed, is that the subject-matter here dealt with has not been heretofore set forth in any one volume.

L. A. Frothingham.

Boston, Massachusetts,
September, 1915.

# CONTENTS

# A BRIEF HISTORY OF THE CONSTITUTION AND GOVERNMENT OF MASSACHUSETTS

# A BRIEF HISTORY OF THE CONSTITUTION AND GOVERNMENT OF MASSACHUSETTS

## CHAPTER I

### EARLY FORMS OF GOVERNMENT

#### The Plymouth Colony

Though the Plymouth Colony lasted as a separate entity less than a century, the founding of the Pilgrim Colony at Plymouth really marks the beginning of Massachusetts history.

This Pilgrim scheme of government and its development are of vital interest to the student of Massachusetts constitutional history. Historians say that the compact signed on board the Mayflower was not a constitution, as it did not create a government, yet that document is nevertheless of vast importance, and far more than a mere historical manuscript. It showed the desire for a government in which every one was to share, and within four months of landing, moreover, a captain was chosen, a treaty with the Indians was concluded, laws and orders were passed, and a governor was elected.

#### The Beginnings of Government

The colonists tried to obtain a charter but never succeeded in doing so. They governed under authority of a patent granted in 1621 by the Council for New England.[1]

[1] This body was established in 1620 by a reorganization of the Plymouth Company. It was given rights of government over all the territories included in its charter. This charter may be found in Ebenezer Hazard's *Historical Collections*, i, p. 103.

In 1629 another patent was granted. All freemen, who were church members, met together as a General Court. Here legislation was enacted, and up to 1636 all trials were also held before this body. In that year, however, the laws were revised, the government established on a permanent basis, the powers of the Governor and Assistants were defined, and the Governor and two Assistants were given certain jurisdiction over trials. This office of Assistant to the Governor had been provided for in 1621, and although at first there was only one Assistant (to succeed the Governor in case of death), the number was gradually increased to seven.

## The General Court

As the settlements increased in number, it was no longer convenient or feasible for all the people to meet as a General Court so deputies were provided for, and in 1639 these deputies were chosen and assembled together from different towns. The towns paid their own delegates and this mode of payment, as we shall see, was customary in Massachusetts. It was not until some time after the adoption of a Constitution in Massachusetts that the burden was taken away from the individual towns and placed upon the state treasury.

The General Court in Plymouth could enact laws but they had to be acted on by two Legislatures, and the freemen could repeal them at the next general election, and enact any other useful measures.[1] What a curious provision this seems to us now! In colonial days we had such safeguards thrown about the enactment of a mere law as are now usually applied only to a constitutional amendment; yet the requirement that an amendment even to such an important

[1] Baylies, *Memoirs of Plymouth Colony*, i, p. 297.

document as the Constitution should be passed by two successive Legislatures is vigorously attacked nowadays as being too lengthy a proceeding.

At the same time, we find in the Plymouth government a species of referendum and initiative which these same critics might applaud. It is often said that there is nothing new under the sun. Here we find an additional confirmation of the truth of that saying. But one cannot find much that is analogous between such a small colony where every one could easily keep in touch with what was going on, and our present-day communities.

### The Courts of the Plymouth Colony

Courts had gradually grown up in the colony with the common law of England as the basis of jurisprudence. As early as 1623 a jury of twelve was provided in cases of criminal facts of trespass and debts. There were four courts — the General Court meeting three times a year, the Court of Assistants also meeting three times a year and trying civil, criminal and appeal cases, a Selectmen's Court for cases under forty shillings between inhabitants of the town, and an Admiralty Court consisting of the Governor and three or four Assistants together with such other substantial persons as the Governor might appoint; and in 1685 — the General Court having divided the colony into counties consisting of Plymouth, Bristol and Barnstable — two County Courts in each county were provided for, to be held by the Assistants.

### The End of the Plymouth Colony

Thus did the system of government grow up and develop in the Pilgrim Colony. What its results might have been had it remained a separate entity, is a matter only of conjecture. We might have today a church government and we might have a government with the initiative and referendum applied on a wide scale. Such suggestions, however, can be but surmises, because under the charter granted by William and Mary establishing the Province of Massachusetts Bay in New England, Plymouth became part of Massachusetts and from that date (1691) her history has been the history of Massachusetts.

Unlike the Plymouth colonists, the men of Massachusetts Bay obtained a charter from the Crown. The original one granted by Charles I established the Governor and Company of Massachusetts Bay, a corporate body composed of a Governor, Deputy-Governor and eighteen Assistants.

## The Colony Charter

Two charters were granted Massachusetts. The first one was given by Charles I, in 1628, and is known as the Colony Charter.[1] Under this charter, the first governor, deputy-governor and assistants were appointed by the Crown. Their successors were to be elected by the freemen of the corporation. The executive power was vested in the governor and assistants and the legislative power in the whole body of the freemen. Considering the opinions on government held by Charles I and his counsellors, it may seem surprising that such a liberal charter was obtained. If this were due to extraordinary enlightenment on their part, it would indeed be surprising. On investigation, however, we find that the charter was granted according to the custom of the times; and we discover many other precedents for such charters. In 1463, for example, a charter was granted by Edward VI to the Merchants Adventurers trading with Flanders. Even as far back as the days of Henry I, in fact,

[1] This may be found in William Macdonald's *Documentary Source Book of American History*, pp. 22–26.

charters were given to merchants guilds. A notable charter was given to the East India Company by Elizabeth in 1599. Thus the charter of 1628 was not an unusual document. This charter and its successor granted under William and Mary were really constitutions. To quote Lord Bryce, a constitution is "a frame of government established by a superior authority creating a subordinate law-making body which can do everything except violate the terms and transcend the powers of the instrument to which it owes its existence." The supreme authority under all charters was the Crown or Parliament. This supreme power passed, when independence was later obtained, not to the legislature but to the people of an independent commonwealth. In a democracy they are the source of all power, the members of the Legislature being elected by them, and consequently their agents.

The charter of 1628 was not brought over to this country by Governor Endicott and the first colonists who settled at Salem. In 1630, however, Winthrop and other settlers reached Salem, and brought the charter with them. Winthrop became Governor both of the company and of the colony. The legal justification for the transfer of this charter was the subject of controversy at the time and has been since. The step was taken, however, with legal advice, and was afterwards sustained in England by court decisions. There was nothing in the charter to prohibit its removal and its presence in Massachusetts was a strong guarantee of the vitality and endurance of the charter as well as of the liberties of those who were to live under it. No one was admitted as a freeman who was not a church member. This regulation continued substantially in force until the downfall of the charter in 1684.

By the terms of the first charter, the principal officers, as we have seen, were to be chosen directly by the freemen. It was agreed at first that the freemen should choose the assistants and that they from among themselves should choose the governor and deputy. This method was too aristocratic, however, to last, and the next spring, in 1631, an order was passed that at least once a year it should be lawful for the people to choose assistants. In 1632, at the next General Court, it was voted that the governor, deputy-governor and the assistants should be chosen every year by this body. This first charter, after safely running the gauntlet of dangers on many occasions, was finally annulled under Charles II in 1684, through *quo warranto* proceedings.

## The Early Courts of Massachusetts Bay.

Courts had gradually grown up in the colony of Massachusetts Bay. At first all judicial matters came before the General Court or before the Court of Assistants, or the Magistrates as they were called, except cases that were cognizable by a justice of the peace. Trial by jury prevailed at first only in cases of murder. In September, 1635, however, grand juries were provided for, and County Courts were established as the population increased. These were composed of Assistants who lived in the county or such others as they could get to sit with them and of citizens nominated by the freemen of the county and approved by the General Court.[1] The idea was to have five in all, any three of whom could hold court. They could try all causes except murder cases or crimes punishable by banishment. Grand and petit juries were summoned to attend them. Appeals could be taken to the Court of Assistants and from them to the General Court. There were petit courts in various towns for the trial of cases of small debts and trespass. In certain

[1] Thomas Hutchinson, *History of Massachusetts*, vol. I, pp. 397–401.

cases, too, where minor offenses had been committed or town by-laws violated, the selectmen had jurisdiction. An admiralty court also existed. The whole arrangement was crude, as may be seen. Though lawyers frequently were elected Assistants, this was not necessarily the case. Even after the establishment of the Superior Court we find a layman as Chief Justice.[1] That the court did not always follow the verdict of the jury is shown by a letter from Mr. Stoughton to the Governor of Plymouth in 1681:

> The testimony you mention against the prisoner I think is clear and sufficient to convict him, but in case your jury should not be of that mind then if you hold yourself strictly obliged by the laws of England no other verdict but 'not guilty' can be brought in, but according to our practice in this jurisdiction we should punish him with some grievous punishment according to the demerit of his crime though not found capital.

## Division of the General Court into Two Bodies

The Court of Assistants, consisting of the Governor, Deputy-Governor and Assistants, met monthly or oftener, while the General Court met four times a year, the Assistants, Governor and Deputy-Governor sitting with them. In the absence of the General Court, the action of the Court of Assistants was given the same force as the action of that body. Laws passed by either were valid when not contrary to the laws of England. Just as in the Plymouth Colony it was found expedient to do away with the practice of having all the freemen meet together in a general court, so in Massachusetts provision was in 1634 made for choosing two or three men to represent the towns. This action was taken partly because the growth of the colony rendered it difficult to transact business with such a large body of men, and partly because the citizens of Watertown protested against

[1] Lieut.-Governor Hutchinson.

a tax levied on them, as they claimed, without their consent. Even after this representative body was established, the Assistants still sat with them as one body and it was not until 1644 that an act was finally passed separating the two bodies so that they henceforth sat apart. Great events seem to be often decided by seemingly trivial occurrences; for according to John Fiske it was owing to a controversy in regard to a stray pig that the Legislature of Massachusetts Bay Colony was divided into two separate bodies.

A stray pig had been impounded by one Captain Keayne, founder and first commander of the Ancient and Honorable Artillery Company, and also donor under his will of a sum of money for the erection of what was the first town-house in Boston. The pig was claimed by a widow named Mrs. Sherman. She brought suit in the law courts without success and then went to the General Court. A majority of the deputies voted in her favor but a majority of the Assistants voted against her. As it was a mooted point whether they sat as one body or as two, the case could never be decided; but it was owing to this controversy, writes Fiske, that an act was later passed providing that the two bodies should sit separately, with co-ordinate jurisdiction.[1]

This makes a very effective story but according to another historian the separation came about because of a division over the request of the people of Newtown to remove to Connecticut.[2] Fifteen of the deputies together with the governor and two of the Assistants were in favor of granting this request while ten deputies and the rest of the Assistants were opposed, "whereupon no record was entered because there were not six assistants in the vote as the patent required." Undoubtedly, there were numerous controversies

[1] John Fiske, *Beginnings of New England*, p. 107.
[2] J. S. Barry, *History of Massachusetts*, First Period, pp. 273, 274.

which led to the final division, and that, after all, is the important thing.

## Establishment of Royal Government

James II, by the appointment of Dudley as Governor, organized the first Royal government of Massachusetts in 1685. Dudley was succeeded the next year by Andros. The Crown gradually took over all colonial governments, both proprietary and charter, except those of Pennsylvania and Maryland on the one hand, and of Rhode Island and Connecticut on the other, though declaring a right to take these as well. From 1684 to 1691 the Massachusetts colony was governed exclusively by these agents of the King, and representative government for the time being ceased to exist.

## The Province Charter

In the year 1691 a new charter was granted the colony by William and Mary. This is commonly known as the Province Charter.[1] Strange to say, it was much less liberal in its terms than the original one granted by Charles I, who was supposed to typify despotic power. The new charter, for instance, took away the right of the colonists to elect their governor, and provided that there should be a Governor, Lieutenant-Governor and secretary appointed by the Crown. It also provided that "in the framing and passing of all such orders, laws, statutes and ordinances and in all elections and acts of government whatsoever to be passed, made or done by the said General Court or Assembly, or in council, the Governor . . . shall have the negative voice." His consent in writing was necessary. Laws were to be sent to England for approval or disapproval, and if not disap-

[1] This may be found in William Macdonald's *Documentary Source Book of American History*, pp. 84–90.

proved within three years after presentation they were to be in force. The Governor was to have command of the militia but he could not grant commissions for the exercising of martial law without the advice and consent of the Council or Assistants. In case of the death or absence of the Governor, the Lieutenant-Governor took his place, and in the absence of both the Governor and the Deputy-Governor, the majority in the Council was in charge of provincial affairs. Admiralty jurisdiction and the creation of admiralty courts were reserved to the Crown. Instead of eighteen Assistants twenty-eight "assistants or counsellors to be advising and assisting to the governor," were provided for. Instead of being chosen by the people they were to be chosen yearly by the General Court or Assembly. Thus the word council came to be used as we find it today, though the Council at this time resembled more our present-day Senate than the Governor's Council as we now know it. It was both a legislative body, acting as an upper house and an advisory body, acting as assistant to the governor.

Under this charter Plymouth, Maine and Nova Scotia became part of Massachusetts. Eighteen at least of the Assistants were to come from what was formerly the colony of Massachusetts Bay, four at least from Plymouth, three at least from what was formerly called the Province of Maine and one at least from the territory lying between the river of Sagadehock and Nova Scotia.

The Councillors, or at least seven of them, were to sit from time to time, when called together by the Governor. A General Court was to be held annually, on the last Wednesday of May, to consist of the Governor and Council and such freeholders as should be elected or deputed by the major part of the freeholders. Each town could elect two representatives and no more, and the General Court was given the right to declare what number each county, town and place should elect. A freehold estate of the value of forty shillings or other estate to the value of forty pounds was the qualification for voting.

## The Distribution of Powers under the Province Charter.

The General Court was empowered to establish courts of record. The Governor, with the advice and consent of the Council or Assistants, had the appointment of judges, commissioners of oyer and terminer, sheriffs, provosts, marshals, justices of the peace and other officers attached to the Council and courts of justice. No such nomination or appointment of officers, however, was to be made without seven days' notice to the Councillors or Assistants.

This Province Charter took away from the Governor and Council all jurisdiction over judicial matters except the probating of wills and granting of administrations. Appeal was given from the courts of the province in any personal action where the matter in dispute was over three hundred pounds, to the King in Privy Council. The General Court was given power to legislate so long as it did not pass laws repugnant to the laws of England. It also was given the power of appointing all civil officers that the Governor and Council did not have the power to appoint. Oaths had to be taken for the faithful performance of their duties by all officers appointed or chosen, as well as the oaths provided by act of Parliament passed in the first year of the King's reign. The Governor was to take the oath before the Lieutenant or Deputy-Governor, or in his absence before any two or more of the Councillors; the Deputy-Governor and the Councillors before the Governor; and all other officers before the

Governor or Deputy-Governor or any two or more of the Councillors.

Under this Province Charter the Governor had power to prorogue or dissolve the General Court, but no power was given the General Court to adjourn itself. This caused dissatisfaction. Disputes had also arisen as to the right of the Governor to veto the election of a Speaker. Governors Dudley and Shute had each put a negative on the election of a Speaker, but the House in each case had refused to acquiesce.[1] Governor Hutchinson vetoed the election of John Hancock as Speaker. To clear up these matters an explanatory charter was granted in 1726 by King George, giving the representatives assembled in any great or general court the right to adjourn not exceeding two days, and also providing that the election of a Speaker should be subject to the approval of the Governor, to be signified by message in writing to the House of Representatives. The right to negative Councillors had seldom been questioned and time and again when active patriots were chosen their election was negatived by the Governor.[2]

## Importance of the Province Charter

The charters granted to Massachusetts and to other colonies are very interesting documents, not only on their own account and as grants of independent legislative power, but because they served as a basis for a future constitution in Massachusetts and in other states. For instance, the provision in the second charter that Councillors were to be elected by the General Court was followed in the Massachusetts Constitution. The people elect them now, but even

[1] Bradford, *History of Plymouth Plantation*, p. 216.

[2] Hutchinson, *History of Massachusetts*, vol. II, pp. 137, 211, 214, 226, and 241.

today, if a vacancy occurs, the General Court if in session fills the vacancy. The provision that a majority of the Council shall run the government in case of the death or absence of the Governor and Lieutenant-Governor, that the Lieutenant-Governor shall succeed the Governor, and that judges be appointed by the Governor with the consent of the Council, were all copied from the Province Charter. The absolute veto given the Governor under that charter and the requirement of the consent of the Council in granting commissions for exercising martial law were placed in the draft submitted by John Adams and the committee to the Convention of 1780. Neither of these provisions was finally put in the Constitution, but they and other clauses of the charter which the people had become used to and found serviceable were utilized in framing our present form of government.

## The Provincial Governor: His Position and Influence

The provincial Governor was a real governor. His powers were vice-regal. He was military head of the government like the king and he could prorogue and dissolve the General Court without being limited by triennial or septennial acts. He could grant charters, like the king, and had the right of pardon. In later years the Assembly learned how to curb these powers. They would hold the Governor in check by granting only a temporary salary, and that often not until he had signed bills which they desired.

As time went on the members of the Assembly began also to direct military affairs. They appointed committees to visit and investigate the army. In 1722 they summoned the commanding officer, Colonel Walton, before them to explain why certain orders of the House had not been carried out. Then by refusing to vote him any pay or to provide for carrying on war they brought about his dismissal. In the same year they forced the Governor to submit to them his speech to the delegates of the Iroquois tribes. They returned it with the proviso that they would agree to it only if delivered in the name of the General Court and in presence of the members of the House. The Governor had to submit.[1]

The power of the Governor of appropriation and of pardon was gradually taken over by the Legislature, and his power of censorship was disputed. It is curious to note the decline of the colonial Governor's power and the usurpation of his authority by the Assembly. It is still more curious to find that the exact opposite has resulted under constitutional government. Under the original constitutions of the states the powers of the Assembly were made paramount and numerous checks placed upon the authority of the Governor. Gradually, however, distrust of legislatures has grown until today we find once more, as in colonial times, a tendency to make the Governor supreme and hold him responsible for the government of the state.

## Relations between Governors and the Assembly

There were constant bickerings between the colonial governors and the Assembly. In spite of the excitement of the times, however, each side seems to have appreciated the position of the other. At least, in their communications they were not constrained from passing on the humor of the situation. In 1770, for instance, there was a dispute between the General Court and the Governor as to the right of the latter to require a sitting in Cambridge or anywhere outside of Boston. Sessions were being held temporarily in

[1] Hutchinson, op. cit., II, pp. 255–260, 265–266.

the Harvard College chapel. The Assembly adopted an address and sent it to the Governor, pointing out, among other things, the inconvenience of sitting in Cambridge, and the Governor replied: "If you think the benefit which the students receive by attending your debates is not equal to what they may gain in their studies, they may easily be restrained, and then your sitting in the College will be little or no inconvenience."

On June 9, 1774, in answer to the speech of General Gage, the newly-appointed Governor, the Council sent this rather pungent reply: "We wish your Excellency every felicity. The greatest of a political nature, both to yourself and the province, is that your administration in the principles and general conduct of it, may be a happy contrast to that of your immediate predecessors." When the chairman of the committee had proceeded thus far with the reading of the reply the Governor stopped him and later sent a message to the Council that he could not receive such an address.

In the same year, by authority of an Act of Parliament and without any action on the part of the General Court, the King appointed thirty-six Councillors by writ of mandamus. Public indignation was aroused to such a point by this action that most of those appointed declined to serve. The new appointees never sat with the General Court. In Worcester one of these mandamus Councillors had to walk through the ranks of some two thousand patriots, reading his resignation. This Act of Parliament also provided that jurors should be selected by the sheriff instead of by the selectmen. It prohibited town meetings, except for the election of officers, without express permission from the Governor.

## Massachusetts Government During the Revolution

The last session of the General Court under the Crown government was held at Salem. On the 17th day of June, 1774, the Governor directed the secretary to declare the General Court dissolved. The secretary went to the court house and found the door of the Representatives' chamber locked. The messenger who reported his presence at the door returned to him with the information that he had acquainted the Speaker with the fact that the secretary had a message from His Excellency, that the Speaker reported the fact to the House, and the orders were to keep the door closed. Soon after this a proclamation dissolving the General Court was published on the stairs leading to the Representatives' chamber in the presence of a group of citizens, some of whom were members of the House. Before dissolving, the General Court elected five delegates to the first Continental Congress. It also made provision for a Provincial Congress with deputies from every town.

This Provincial Congress organized at Salem on October 7, 1774, and after electing John Hancock president immediately adjourned to meet at Concord. It met at Concord from October 11th to the 14th, then at Cambridge from the 17th to the 29th, and again in Cambridge from November 23d to December 10th, with closed doors, dissolving on December 10th. The second Provincial Congress met at Cambridge on the 1st of February, 1775, sat there, at Concord, and at Watertown, adjourning at the latter place on the 29th of May. The third Provincial Congress met on the 31st day of May at Watertown. Joseph Warren was chosen president in the place of Hancock, and on July 19th it dissolved.

The Provincial Congress sat without a Governor. The Council of twenty-eight was continued and sat during the Revolutionary War and until the adoption of the Constitution, taking the place of the chief executive. Thus, with the Provincial Congress, town meetings, a Council, committees of safety, and finally a General Court meeting on July 26, 1775, at the suggestion of the Continental Congress, Massachusetts was governed up to the time of the adoption of the constitution.

## Events Leading up to the Adoption of a Constitution

Massachusetts was the last of the original thirteen states to adopt a constitution; but she was the first state to submit her constitution to a vote of the people. The events leading up to the adoption of a constitution by Massachusetts are of great interest.

The Council had proceeded to reorganize the courts and to grant commissions, but this temporary makeshift did not work well. Many of the people were oppressed by debts; in places they interfered with the sittings of the inferior courts. There were contentions, too, between the Council and the House. In Berkshire County no state courts were allowed. The towns ran things themselves. Pittsfield, for instance, named five men to sit and hold a local court. The citizens of Lee voted that they held themselves "bound to support the civil authority of this state for the term of one year and bound to obey the laws of this state," and Great Barrington voted "No" on the question "Whether, under the situation of this county, not having a new constitution, and other reasons, the laws of the state are to operate among us."

Some of the votes passed by town meetings during this critical period are both interesting and significant. For example, the town of Ashfield voted (October 4, 1774),—

> That we will take the law of God for the foundation of the forme of our Government . . . that it is our opinion that we do not want any Govinor but the Govinor of the Universe & under him a States General to consult with wrest of the U. S. for the good of the whole — that the Assembly of this State consist of one Elective body, the members of which body shall be Annually elected — that all Acts passed by the General Court of the State respecting the several towns be sent to the several towns for their acceptance before they shall be in force . . . that it is our opinion that each town is invested with a native authority to chuse a Committee or Number of Judges consisting of a number of understanding & prudent men that shall jug & determine all cases between man & man, setel Intestate estates, & collect all debts that have been contracted or may be contracted within their Limits & all Controversies whatsoever except in the case of murder & then it will be necessary to call in eleven men from eleven neiboring Towns that shall be cose (chosen?) for that purpose annually to jug & condemn such murderers.

Other towns also took the initiative in proposing a new scheme of state government. The town of Stoughton, in October, 1776, proposed (*a*) that county conventions should each draft a form of government for the state, and (*b*) that a state convention should be made up of these county conventions or of delegates selected by them. The town of Bellingham, also proposed an elaborate plan of district conventions which should make drafts and report back to the towns, to be followed by a general committee made up of one member from each district.

Pittsfield likewise began to agitate the matter. There a petition was circulated and the Reverend Thomas Allen declared that all he wanted was a government founded on the consent of the people. This was the same reverend gentleman who was known as "the fighting parson" and who led his congregation to Bennington and complained to

Colonel Stark, the night before that celebrated battle, that he had been disappointed on several occasions and did not want to miss a fight this time. Colonel Stark assured him that he would have all the fighting he wanted on the morrow, and the reverend gentleman presumably did.

### The First Proposal (1778) Rejected

In view of all this unrest and agitation the House of Representatives, in 1776, appointed a committee to take under consideration the matter of a constitution, and, later, the House resolved to recommend to the towns to vote, first, whether they would empower the House and the Council as a joint body to consult, agree, and enact a constitution; and, second, whether it should be published for the inspection and perusal of the inhabitants before the ratification thereof by the Assembly. There were 250 towns in the state. Of these only ninety-seven made returns; seventy-four of these were in favor of the propositions; twenty-three including Boston, were against. As a result of this, four members of the Council and eight of the House were appointed, and submitted a draft of a constitution. Unfortunately, the journals of the House and Council throw no information on the proceedings. Suffice it to say however, that a form was agreed upon, and, on the 4th of March, 1778, submitted to the people with the provision that the assent of two-thirds of the people should be required for the adoption of the constitution. One hundred and twenty towns neglected to express any opinion. Five-sixths of those expressing an opinion voted in the negative, including Boston. The constitution was rejected by some 10,000 to 2,000 or a vote of five to one.

There were various reasons for this action. Some thought that a special convention should be called to draw up such an important document; others that it was wiser to wait for more tranquil times; some objected that no bill of rights had been inserted; others that there was not a proper separation of the executive and the legislative functions.[1] Many of the ablest men, too, were away from the state, attending the Continental Congress.

## Continuance of the Agitation

On the rejection of this constitution the agitation throughout the colony started anew. There was almost open rebellion, the illegal nature of the existing government being given as a reason. Some of the officers were still royalists and this intensified the feeling against the courts. The Reverend Mr. Allen of Pittsfield was a leader. A petition to the General Court was drawn up, in which objections were made to the debtors' law and the assumption of power by the General Court. The localities wanted to elect their own judges. Courts were repeatedly prevented from sitting. The towns to a great extent ran things themselves. The towns in several cases (Pittsfield, Lenox and Hancock), voted that they were not bound to obey state laws. Threats of separation were made. The state government was practically suspended. In Berkshire they petitioned for a constitutional convention, suggesting that "if this honorable court are for dismembering, there are other states, which

[1] "We see also something of the political character of a Hill Town in the suggestions which *Warwick* makes to its representative. They desire that the Legislature shall consist of *one chamber* (one of the coast towns was about the same time instructing its members to make sure that there were two chambers) that each town shall have one member, towns of the largest class not more than 4 or 5, the rest in proportion, that suffrage shall be universal, that a town shall have the right to *recall* its member at any time on evidence of misconduct, and that at no time shall less than 80 members constitute a house." Jameson, *Introduction to the History of the States*, p. 25.

have constitutions which will,we doubt not,as bad as we are, gladly receive us." Its representatives were instructed to demand a new constitution. The final adoption of the constitution may have prevented Berkshire from today being part of the State of New York. At any rate, the Berkshire constitutionalists helped materially to give us a constitution in Massachusetts.

The sea towns in Essex County took a lively interest in political affairs. Here the proposed constitution of 1778 was rejected. At Newburyport the town voted that the selectmen write circular letters to the towns in the county suggesting a convention of delegates to consider the proposed constitution. As a result, some of the most prominent citizens assembled at Treadwell's Tavern in Ipswich. Here a minute and critical examination of the clauses of the proposed constitution was instituted. The various objections made to the constitution and suggestions of what such a document should contain were drawn up by Theophilus Parsons and printed at Newburyport in the form of a pamphlet. It was entitled "The Result of the Ipswich Convention." This pamphlet not only had much influence upon the decision of the towns in rejecting the constitution proposed at that time, but also, by its suggestions, was of great assistance in drafting the constitution finally adopted.

Before taking up that constitution it will be interesting to note some of the provisions of the rejected one. Of course I shall cite only some of its most striking clauses.

Under it, the Governor and Lieutenant-Governor were to be members of the Senate, the Governor being President of this body. The Senate was to consist of twenty-eight members, exclusive of the Governor and Lieutenant-Governor. Vacancies in the Senate were to be filled by the House, which was to be made up of representatives from the towns.

In case of the death or absence of both the Governor and Lieutenant-Governor, the Senate was to succeed to their powers. In matters requiring the action of the Governor and Senate no veto was given the Governor. The power of pardon was placed with the Governor, Lieutenant-Governor and Speaker. Only Protestants could be Governor, Lieutenant-Governor, Senator, Representative or Judge.

Curiously enough, none of these special provisions were inserted in the constitution adopted two years later, but a great deal of the work bestowed on the document proved valuable to the framers of the next one.

# CHAPTER II

## THE CONSTITUTION OF MASSACHUSETTS

On the 19th of February, 1779, the Legislature adopted a resolution providing for a vote of the people on two questions: (1) "Whether the people would choose at this time to have any new form of government at all"; (2) "Whether in case they did they would empower their representatives to summon an assembly for the sole purpose of preparing such a form."

Though nearly half of the towns neglected to answer these questions, a majority of the rest responded in the affirmative. An election of delegates was accordingly held, and on September first they assembled at Cambridge. The meeting-place was the old church which stood near the site now occupied by Dane Hall. James Bowdoin was chosen President of the Convention. It was voted to have a bill of rights; that the government to be framed by the Convention should be a free republic, and that "it is of the essence of a free republic that the people be governed by fixed laws of their own making." A grand committee of thirty was appointed to draft a constitution.

### The Work of John Adams

The Convention then adjourned to October 28. The grand committee met and appointed James Bowdoin, Samuel Adams, and John Adams a sub-committee of three. This sub-committee delegated the preparation of the draft to John Adams. Mr. Adams performed the task allotted to him. He had given these matters great thought and made suggestions at the request of other colonies in relation to drawing up their constitutions. He had even submitted plans for them. He was undoubtedly the man best fitted for the work. In a letter he says: "There never was an example of such precautions as are taken by these wise and jealous people in the formation of their government. None was ever made so perfectly upon the principle of the people's rights and equality. It is Locke, Sidney, and Rousseau and DeMably reduced to practice, in the first instance. I wish every step of their progress printed and preserved."[1] In a letter to Mr. Jennings dated June 7, 1780, he says: "I was chosen by my native town into the Convention two or three days after my arrival. I was by the Convention put upon the committee; by the committee upon the sub-committee; so that I had the honor to be principal engineer. The committee made some alterations, as, I am informed, the Convention have made a few others in the report; but the frame and essence and substance is preserved."[2]

The task of drafting the bill of rights was left by the general committee to Mr. Adams alone. This was reported by him to the Convention with the exception of the third article which he seems to have thought could be better drawn up by some of the clergy.

On October 28th, the Convention re-assembled, and on November 11th it adjourned to meet in Boston on the 5th of January, 1780.

Some changes were made by the Convention in the draft submitted to them. For instance, Mr. Adams' draft provided for an absolute veto by the Governor without any provision for the Legislature to over-ride it. This was drastic, especially as in some of the states the Governor was

[1] C. F. Adams, *Life and Works of John Adams*, vol. iv, p. 216.

[2] *Ibid.*

given no veto at all. Mr Adams provided that no man should be eligible as Governor more than five years in any seven. He did not give to the House of Representatives the privilege of asking opinions from the Supreme Court, but restricted that right to the Governor and Council and to the Senate. He provided that the Senate, and not the Governor and Council, should hear causes of marriage, divorce and alimony "until the Legislature shall by law make other provision." All officers of the militia were to be appointed by the Governor with the advice and consent of the Council. This, too, was changed by the Convention, thus making, according to Mr. Adams, the second material change in his draft, that concerning the absolute veto of the Governor being the first.[1]

### The New Constitution Submitted and Accepted

On the 2d of March, 1780, the Constitution[2] was finally agreed to and submitted to the people, together with an address defending and explaining the document. The Convention then adjourned, to meet on the 7th of June, at the Brattle Street Church in Boston, where the votes for and against the adoption of the Constitution were to be counted. A two-thirds vote was required for adoption, and it having been ascertained that the requisite number of votes had been obtained, a resolve was adopted for carrying the Constitution into effect and the Convention dissolved on the 16th of June.

The first General Court under the new frame of government met at the State House in Boston on the 25th of October of the same year. It consisted of two hundred mem-

[1] *Life and Works of John Adams*, pp. 231, n. 1; 249, n. 1.

[2] A copy of this document, as finally agreed upon, may be found in the *Manual for the General Court*, published annually by the Commonwealth.

bers. The condition of the country was still unsettled and serious opposition tended to frustrate the proper workings of the government. Criticisms were made of the aristocratic character of the Senate, of the independent Executive, and his salary, of the courts, until finally in 1786 an armed revolt known as Shays's Rebellion broke out, threatening the very existence of the new government. This uprising was suppressed, however, and as time went on and the workings of the government under this Constitution were found to be practical and efficient, acquiescence in the scheme and belief in its broad provisions became stronger and stronger. Less turbulent and more prosperous times were in sight and from condemnation and criticism almost universal praise arose for the system of government.

## The Constitution of 1780 still in Force

Forty-four amendments have been made to the Massachusetts Constitution and two Constitutional Conventions have been held since the one we have been discussing, yet the Constitution of 1780 is still in force. The original Constitution in practically all the states of the Union has been superseded by at least one, and in most cases by several new documents, each one growing longer and laying down provisions relating to an infinite number of subjects. Massachusetts alone is living under her original Constitution. This has been possible because of the provisions for amendment and because of the liberal enactments in the original document. It is not because Massachusetts is behind the times, but because the originators of her constitution were far-seeing enough to draw up a liberal and flexible document. The length of time it has lasted and the satisfaction it has given, the great industries that have grown up under it, the prosperity and happiness of the people, the advancement of science and education,— all stand as bright tributes to the master minds that originated the Constitution and carried it to successful adoption one hundred and thirty-five years ago.

### Some of its Distinctive Features

It would be impossible in this short treatise to explain everything contained in this Constitution. On some of the phases which differentiate it from the constitutions of other states and which seem to me of particular importance, however, I wish to touch.

In many of the original constitutions of the various states the judges and state officers, with the exception of the Governor, were elected by the Legislature. Even today in some of them we find provisions for electing various state officers by the Legislature instead of directly by the people. Under the Massachusetts Constitution of 1780, it was provided that the Secretary, Treasurer and Receiver-General, the Commissary-General and Notaries Public should be chosen annually by joint ballot of the Senators and Representatives, and this method of election of state officers prevailed up to 1855 when it was changed by amendment so that they should be chosen directly by the people. The office of notary ceased to be elective in 1820, Article 4 of the Amendments providing that notaries should be appointed by the Governor as were other judicial officers, except that their term should be for seven years and not for life. In New Jersey, Maryland, Virginia, North and South Carolina, Pennsylvania, and Delaware, under the original constitutions the chief executive was elected on joint ballot by the two houses of the Legislature.

The Virginia plan for a Constitution of the United States, moreover, provided that the executive branch of the government should be placed in the hands of a single man to be chosen by the Legislature. This Governor or President was to hold office for a short term and to be ineligible for re-election. The judges of the Supreme Court, also, were to be chosen by the Legislature. These ideas did not find favor in Massachusetts. Yearly sessions of the Legislature were provided for and though there have been attempts to have biennial sessions Massachusetts continues to be one of the six States of the Union whose Legislature meets annually. It is the only State that has both annual sessions and annual elections of its state officers. There are only three other States in the Union which have a Governor's Council.[1] There are a number of States that have no Lieutenant-Governor, and in States where they do have one, there being no Council he is apt to preside over the Senate as the Vice-President does in Washington. The power of appointment, too, in most States is subject to ratification by the Senate, and not, as in Massachusetts, by the Council. Either branch of the Legislature or the Governor and Council may require the opinions of the justices of the Supreme Court on important questions of law and on solemn occasions.[2] This is an unusual privilege, and according to Mr. Stimson it is allowed only in six other States and in two of those it is limited either to important questions of law or to those concerning the State Constitution.[3] Many of the far-seeing and liberal provisions contained in the Constitution I shall take up later, but two more I shall refer to now.

[1] These are Maine, New Hampshire and North Carolina.

[2] See below, Chap. IV.

[3] Stimson, *Federal and State Constitutions of the United States*, §652, n. 6.

## Some Special Provisions of the Constitution

### (1) Limitation of Martial Law

Within the last two years we have read of committees from Washington visiting the State of West Virginia to investigate a strike of coal miners which was in progress there. Martial law had been declared, and the Supreme Court of Appeals of that State, with one judge dissenting, held that martial law could be declared by the Governor, and that the question as to necessity lay with him, that a military court could properly try men for offenses committed, though it was shown that some civil courts were open in other parts of the same county before which the men might have been taken for trial.[1] Such action as this revolutionizes the generally accepted doctrine as to martial law in this country, and it would certainly surprise and outrage people in Massachusetts if the Governor could in his own discretion declare martial law and supersede the civil courts and government by military tribunals. The founders of that state government, however, were cognizant of the possibilities of abuse through martial law and the suspension of the writ of habeas corpus; consequently they provided in her bill of rights that "no person can in any case be subject to law-martial or to any penalties or pains by virtue of that law except those employed in the Army or Navy and except the militia in actual service but by authority of the Legislature."[2]

This provision is far broader than one merely restricting the power to call out the militia of the State. There is a radical difference between calling out the militia to suppress a tumult or riot and the application of martial law to the

[1] 71 *W. Va.*, 519.

[2] *Massachusetts Constitution*, Part I, Art. XXVIII.

civil population. In Massachusetts the laws give the power of calling out the militia in cases of riot not only to the Governor but to mayors, sheriffs and the selectmen of towns as well.[1] Martial law can be applied to civilians in Massachusetts only by vote of the Legislature, and this restriction is found in the constitutions of only two other States, namely New Hampshire and South Carolina.[2] It is, nevertheless, a safeguard that all the States might well adopt. A power left to the discretion of two representative bodies of the people is much less apt to be abused than one dependent upon the decision of a single man.

In the last chapter of the Constitution it was further provided that the writ of habeas corpus shall only be suspended by the Legislature upon the most urgent and pressing occasions, and for a time not exceeding twelve months.[3]

### (2) The Removal of Judges by Address

Under the Massachusetts Constitution judges are appointed for life. Great stress was laid by Mr. Adams in the Convention, on the importance of this method of tenure for judges and it was finally adopted. While all the state officers, including judges, can be removed under the Constitution by impeachment, there is a particular provision, and a very interesting one, providing that judges can be removed by the Governor on address of the two Houses of the Legislature with the consent of the Council. This broad power of removal by address although long existent in England is so unusual in this country and so important that it requires a detailed explanation.

[1] *Revised Laws of Massachusetts*, Chap. 16, § 121. See also, 5 Gray (*Mass.*), 121.

[2] Stimson, op. cit., § 293, n. 4.

[3] *Constitution of Massachusetts*, Chap. vi, Art. vii.

When Colonel Roosevelt said in his famous speech before the Ohio Constitutional Convention at Columbus, speaking of the recall of judges, that he favored such a *drastic* method of removal of judges as was embodied in the Massachusetts Constitution, many people opened their eyes with amazement. Few, of course, had heard of removal by address, and fewer still, if they had heard of it, understood what was meant. This is quite natural as no case of removal by address has taken place in Massachusetts since 1882.

Constitutions are generally supposed to be dull things and few people, I think, read them even in these times when it is so common to attack their provisions. The fact remains, however, that in the old Bay State there exists a most effective and unusually liberal system for the speedy removal of judges.

Among the States of the Union that provide for removal by address, the greater number stipulate that a two-thirds vote of both the House and the Senate is necessary in order to remove the judge; in Massachusetts a bare majority vote of each House is sufficient. In most States the cause of the proposed removal of a judge must be stated; notice must also be served on the accused, and a hearing given; but under the requirements of the Massachusetts Constitution no reason need be assigned and no hearing is necessary.

Daniel Webster, speaking of this subject before the Convention of 1820, assumed that removal could take place without trial or accusation. He said, "If the judges, in fact, hold their office only so long as the Legislature sees fit, then it is vain and illusory to say that the judges are independent men incapable of being influenced by hope or by fear; but the tenure of their office is not independent. The general theory and principle of the Government is broken in upon by giving the Legislature this power. The departments of Government are not equal, co-ordinate and independent while one is thus at the mercy of the others. What would be said of a proposition to authorize the Governor or Judges to remove a Senator or member of the House of Representatives from office?" And Lemuel Shaw, afterwards Chief Justice of Massachusetts, said in addressing the Convention: "By the Constitution as it stands, the judges hold their offices at the will of the majority of the Legislature."

## How This Provision Has Worked

There has been much dispute as to whether this clause for removal of judges by address in the Constitution of Massachusetts extended any further than to cover removal for incapacity. It was because of incapacity that Judge Bradbury was removed by address in 1803. He had become enfeebled by old age and unfit to do his work.

Let us glance at some of the cases which have arisen in Massachusetts. There have been a number of them. Besides Mr. Justice Bradbury, two judges of the Court of Common Pleas were removed by address in 1803 for extortion in office and two justices of the peace in 1876. The most famous cases, however, are those of Mr. Loring, Judge of the Probate Court for the County of Suffolk, and of Mr. Day, Judge of the Probate Court of the County of Barnstable. In both these latter cases hearings were given. This was the general custom. The course of procedure followed the usual method governing legislation. A petition was introduced in both cases for the removal of these judges. The petition was referred to a joint committee,— in the Loring case to the Committee on Federal Relations, and in the Day case to a special committee. These committees then sat and heard the evidence for and against removal, and also the arguments of counsel, after which in due course they reported to the House or Senate. This report, of course, had to be acted upon by both bodies. If the committee favored removal they said so at the end of the report, then they further recommended that a joint committee, consisting of two on the part of the Senate and five on the part of the House be appointed to present the address to the Governor. Full reasons for the removal were given in the report of the Committees, and if there were dissenters they were allowed to file a report of their own. When the House and the Senate adopted the report the address was taken by this special Committee to the Governor. In the case of Judge Loring, the address read as follows: "The two branches of the Legislature in General Court assembled, respectfully request that your Excellency would be pleased by and with the advice and consent of the Council, to remove Edward Greely Loring from the office of Judge of the Probate Court for the County of Suffolk."

When the address reaches the Governor it consists merely of a request for the removal of the judge, and does not state any reasons as does the report of the Legislative Committee. The Governor after the receipt of the address presents the question of removal to the Council, and if the Council and the Governor favor removal the latter issues a writ of removal, sending a message to the Legislature informing them of the fact that removal has taken place.

In both of these cases the first attempt at removal was unsuccessful. Judge Loring was not only Judge of Probate, but also held a commission from the Federal Government as United States Commissioner. In the latter capacity he signed a warrant for the rendition of the negro fugitive, Anthony Burns. This act created a furore. The Legislature was appealed to by Judge Loring's opponents. Long hearings were held at which distinguished counsel represented both sides, and in the end the two Houses voted an address to the Governor and Council. Governor Gardner, however, sent a message back to the Legislature refusing to remove Judge Loring. This was in 1855. During the remainder of that year and during 1856 no further address was sent to the Governor. But in 1857, although an adverse report was made by the committee on federal relations with one dissenter on the petitions for the removal by address of Judge Loring,[1] this report was substituted in the Senate by a vote of twenty to fifteen and then the address with amendments was adopted by a vote of twenty-five to twelve.[2] The House, on the 20th of May, adopted the address by a vote of two hundred and ten to sixty-nine.[3] A joint committee was duly appointed to deliver the address. They reported back that its members had performed their duty. The Governor sent an answer, which was a very brief one as the House was about to adjourn, refusing to remove Judge Loring, but later sent an elaborate message giving full reasons for his refusal to comply with the address.[4]

In this second address to Governor Gardner reasons were given for asking for the removal of Judge Loring, as follow:

1. Because he consented to sit as United States Slave Commissioner in defiance of the moral sentiment of Massachusetts as expressed in the Legislative Resolves of 1850.
2. Because, now, in defiance of the provisions contained in section 13 of Chapter 489 of the Acts of 1855, Edward G. Loring continues to hold the office of judge of probate, under a Massachusetts commission, and at the same time to hold in defiance of law a commission under the United States, which qualifies him to issue warrants and grant certificates, under the Act of Congress named in the 9th section of Chapter 489 of the Acts of 1855.

[1] *Senate Journal*, 1857, p. 513.
[2] *Ibid.*, pp. 610–612.
[3] *House Journal*, 1857, p. 716.
[4] *Massachusetts Acts and Resolves*, Special Messages, 1856–57.

In 1858 Governor Banks took office, and the Legislature after extended hearings sent an address to him requesting the removal of Judge Loring as Judge of Probate. Governor Banks acceded to the request and removed the Judge, on the ground that an act had been passed by the Legislature making it illegal for one man to occupy the two offices.

No reasons were assigned in the first or last of these three addresses; but in their messages both Governor Gardner and Governor Banks gave their reasons,—in one for not removing, and in the other for removing the Judge.[1]

In the other case, that of Mr. Justice Day, several hearings were held and all the accusations against him were thoroughly investigated. In 1881 when the case came up for the first time, the committee reported against removing him and their report was sustained by the Legislature. In 1882, however, the committee reported in favor of removal; both Houses voted for it, and the Governor removed Judge Day accordingly. No reasons were given by the Legislature in its address to the Governor and none were given by the latter in acceding to the request for removal.[2] Even as late as this case, a petition was signed by leading members of the bar, asking that the opinion of the Supreme Court be requested as to the right of removal by address for any cause except mental or physical incapacity. This suggestion, however, was not acted upon.

Whatever the intention of the framers of the Constitution may have been, there seems no doubt from the language used, which is without limitation, that the right of removal by address is quite unrestricted. This particular clause, however, like many others, was taken from the British sys-

[1] *House Document*, No. 302, 1855; *House Document*, No. 107, 1858; *Senate Document*, No. 84, 1858.

[2] *Senate Document*, No. 200, 1881, and *Senate Document*, No. 150, 1882.

tem of government, where, instead of the original power of the King to remove judges, the Act of Settlement at the time of William and Mary provided that they could be removed by the King on address made to him by Parliament. No hearing was provided for and no restriction was placed on the cause of removal. The power of the King arbitrarily and alone to remove judges was taken from him,— that was all. As in Great Britain a hearing has been usual on petitions for removal by address so in Massachusetts the justice of the people and their demand for fair play will ever avail to secure the accused a hearing. Few cases have arisen in either jurisdiction. Where a serious offense is charged, impeachment is the natural method of procedure. But so far as precedent goes, a hearing is customary, and any cause may be alleged (not alone disability) to justify removal by address.

### The Right of Removal by Address and the Recall of Judges

Because the judges in Massachusetts have so seldom abused their power; because the people feel that they are men of uprightness and great learning; because they know that only through stability and security of tenure of office, regardless of fear, of political cliques and parties, can justice be maintained; because of the liberal method of removing judges provided in its Constitution, there has not been, nor do I think there is today, any popular demand either for the recall of judges or of judicial decisions in that Commonwealth. Strange to say, it has been in States where judges are elected that the complaints against their decisions have arisen. There have been too many examples of the viciousness of this policy of having judges dependent for their positions on the bidding of political chiefs to warrant taking the risk of extending the system. The solution would seem to lie in such liberal provisions as exist in the Constitution of Massachusetts.

The recall of judges is not a new idea. It was suggested and even vigorously applied in this country even before the adoption of the United States Constitution. In the years between the Revolution and the adoption of this Constitution, each State issued paper money. "The paper currency showed an immediate tendency to drop to two cents or thereabouts on the dollar. Mutton chops could sometimes be obtained for $4 apiece and a good wearable hat for $40; but more usually a prudent shopkeeper preferred to lose his customer than handle such precarious stuff. Clearly something was wrong and the people taking thought discovered that it was the shopkeepers who needed coercion. Laws accordingly were passed with this object, and when they were defied, the matter came before the Courts. The Judges sitting amid the noisy demonstration of popular anger, decided nevertheless that the laws were invalid and absolved the defendants. Up to this time there had been if not unanimity at any rate a huge majority supporting the panacea; but now there was a division. One party grumbled but owned itself defeated; the other with a stern logic discovered that to complete the system the judges must be done away with or intimidated. In Rhode Island they were accordingly dismissed, and elsewhere there was dangerous rioting. In Massachusetts there was civil war."[1]

[1] F. S. Oliver, *Life of Alexander Hamilton*, p. 136.

# CHAPTER III

## THE CONSTITUTIONAL CONVENTION OF 1820

There have been two Constitutional Conventions in Massachusetts since the adoption of the state Constitution in 1780. One was held in 1820; the other in 1853. In 1820 the separation of Maine from Massachusetts, the excessive number of members in the House of Representatives, the existing system of apportionment of Senators, and objections to the third article of the Bill of Rights, made it seem desirable to amend the Constitution. The Legislature accordingly submitted to the people the question of calling a convention for this purpose and the people voted in favor of such a step. This first convention (1820) sat fifty-five days, Sundays included, and the second (1853) sat three months.

The Constitution as adopted in 1780 required a two-thirds vote of the people for its adoption. So did the proposed Constitution of 1778, which was rejected, as it failed to receive a two-thirds vote. The Constitution of 1780 also provided for amendment by the people in the year 1795, if they so decreed by a two-thirds vote. They did not so decree and consequently no delegates were elected to meet in convention for that purpose. It is interesting to note, however, that neither the convention of 1820 nor that of 1853 provided for a two-thirds vote to adopt the proposals put forward by them.

### Personnel and Work of the Convention

The Convention of 1820 met at the State House in Boston on the 15th of November. Many men of great distinction sat in it. The names of Webster, Shaw, Adams, Morton, Pickman and Story, for example, appear prominently on its records.

Fourteen amendments were adopted and submitted to the people. Five of these were rejected and the other nine form the first nine amendments to the Constitution of Massachusetts.

## The Rejected Amendments

The first article was rejected. It provided that the power and duty of the Legislature to make provision for public worship and the support of public teachers of religion should not be confined to incorporated societies or to Protestant teachers but should extend to all public Christian teachers of piety, religion and morality; that the clause in the third article of the Declaration of Rights which invests the Legislature with power to require compulsory church attendance be annulled, and that no person should be tried for a crime or offense involving imprisonment or ignominious punishment except on indictment by a grand jury unless provided otherwise expressly by statute and every one was to be entitled to a hearing in his own defense by himself and counsel. The latter was hardly germane to the first two subjects dealt with. The people rejected this article by a majority of over 8,000. Twelve years later, in 1833, however, the important part of the provision relating to public worship was put before the voters in better form, and adopted as an amendment to the Constitution.[1]

Article 2 was also rejected. It provided for a change of the political year from May to January, and of the election day from May to November. This was defeated by a little over 2,500 votes.

[1] *Constitution of Mass.*, Article of Amendment XI.

Article 5 provided for the election of thirty-six Senators instead of forty, for a Council of seven, elected by joint ballot from the people at large (excluding members of the House and Senate), for a new apportionment of the House of Representatives, still keeping it altogether too large, however, as the convention did not want to take away representation from the small towns, and for paying Representatives from the treasury of the Commonwealth instead of from that of the towns. This article was rejected by a majority of over 10,800.

The political year was changed eleven years later, from the last Wednesday of May to the first Wednesday of January, and in 1855 another amendment made the first Tuesday after the first Monday in November election day.[1] In the same way the provisions relating to the election of members of the Senate, the Council and the House of Representatives were changed by individual amendments. It was so difficult to arrive, however, at any satisfactory basis of representation in the House, that it took three more amendments, one in the year 1836,[2] another in 1840,[3] and a final one in 1857,[4] to reach the present basis,— a House of two hundred and forty members distributed in districts according to the number of voters. An amendment was adopted in 1840 providing for a Senate of forty from the then existing senatorial districts, the Governor and Council to assign the number of Senators from each district according to the number of inhabitants in the district.[5] In 1857 a final amendment was passed providing for the election of forty Senators from as many districts, each district to contain as nearly as may

[1] *Constitution of Massachusetts*, Articles of Amendment X and XV.

[2] *Ibid.*, XII.

[3] *Ibid.*, XIII.

[4] *Ibid.*, XXI.

[5] *Ibid.*, XIII.

be an equal number of voters.[1] Time, too, was required to arrive at the present basis of election to the Governor's Council. A change was made in 1840 whereby nine Councillors were to be chosen from the people at large by joint ballot of the Senators and Representatives.[2] This system was again changed by the passage of another amendment in 1855 providing for election by the people of eight Councillors, one from each district.[3] This is the method now in vogue.

The clause looking to the payment of Representatives out of the treasury of the Commonwealth was not renewed by constitutional amendment. In 1893 an amendment was adopted annulling the provision in the Constitution that the expenses of legislators going to and returning from the General Court should be paid once and no more out of the treasury of the Commonwealth.[4] But long before this a statute had been passed providing that travelling expenses as well as pay of members should come out of the public treasury[5] and there seems to have been no legal reason for having a constitutional amendment on the subject at any time.[6] It was apparently inserted in 1820 as a sop to the small towns for having their representation cut down.[7]

There were two other articles submitted by the convention of 1820 which were rejected by the people. One of them, the ninth, provided for the removal of justices of the peace by address,[8] restricted the removal of any judicial

[1] *Constitution of Massachusetts*, Article of Amendment XXII.
[2] *Ibid.*, XIII. [3] *Ibid.*, XVI. [4] *Ibid.*, XXXV.
[5] In 1858. See *Revised Laws*, Chap. 3, § 8; *Acts 1911*, Chap. 676.
[6] I *Opinions of the Attorney-General*, p. 42.
[7] *Journal of the Constitutional Convention*, 1820, pp. 514–518.
[8] There was some doubt as to whether this power already existed. *Ibid.*, p. 490.

officer by address until the causes of removal were first stated by entry on the Journal of the House in which it originated, and a copy served on the accused so that he might be admitted to a hearing in his defense, and took away from the Governor and Council and the two branches of the Legislature the right to require opinions from the Judges of the Supreme Court.

To the first part of this article there could have been no particular objection. In fact, a much easier method of removing justices of the peace was adopted by amendment to the Constitution in 1907, when it was provided that the Governor with the consent of the Council, might himself remove justices of the peace and notaries public.[1] The second part requiring a hearing before removal of a judge by address must also have seemed fair. The whole article was probably rendered abortive by the addition of the last paragraph abolishing the right to ask opinions of the Supreme Court.

Joseph Story of Salem was chairman of the Committee on the Judiciary in the Convention. In their original report the committee suggested that removal by address be subject not to a majority but to a two-thirds vote of the members present in each branch of the Legislature. The Committee's report favoring a two-thirds majority for removal was beaten in the Convention by a vote of two hundred and ten to one hundred and five, and the next day a motion was made by Daniel Webster[2] wording the amendment as it was finally submitted to the people, but even in that form it was voted down with the rest of the article by a majority of over 2,000.

[1] *Constitution of Massachusetts*, Article of Amendment XXXVII.

[2] *Journal of the Convention*, 1820, p. 489.

The statement issued by the Convention to the people in relation to the last clause of this article is interesting. It shows the reasons for its insertion. "No opinion," they say, "ought to be formed and expressed by any judicial officer affecting the interest of any citizen but upon a full hearing according to law . . . each department ought to act on its own responsibility . . . judges may be called on to give opinions on subjects which may afterward be drawn into judicial examination before them by contending parties," and "if the question proposed should be of a public nature it will be likely to partake of a political character; and it highly concerns the people that judicial officers should not be involved in political or party discussions." [1]

The other article rejected by the people related to Harvard College. It was numbered Article 10, and provided that the Board of Overseers, in the election of ministers to the Board, should not be restricted to ministers of churches of any particular denomination of Christians.[2] This article, strange to say, was negatived by a vote of over 12,000. The subject matter was subsequently dealt with by an Act of the Legislature.[3]

## THE ACCEPTED AMENDMENTS

This convention was of great importance both in the notable and able discussions that took place, preserving for us the views of men of learning and great distinction, and also from the fact that nine of the amendments emanating from it were adopted. I shall not discuss these amendments at length as this is not a history of the convention.

[1] *Journal of the Convention*, 1820, p. 629.
[2] *Ibid.*, p. 631 and reference in note.
[3] *Constitution of Massachusetts*, Article III of Chap. V, reserved to the Legislature this right.

One of the most significant was the last article which provided for future amendments to the Constitution. This stipulates, as we know, that a proposed amendment to become effective must be passed by two successive Legislatures and then adopted by the people. Unlike the provision in the Constitution for over-riding a veto, however, which requires a vote of two-thirds of the members of each body, a constitutional amendment, though it must be voted for by two-thirds of the members of the House of Representatives present and voting thereon, requires only a majority vote of the Senate. The reason for this may be summed up in a few words, from the remarks of Daniel Webster on page 414 of the Journal of the Massachusetts Convention of 1820, where he says, "It has been heard repeatedly in debate, that if the Senate was organized in the manner proposed, and two-thirds of the Senate are required to assent to any amendment, it would be in the power of less than one-third of the people to defeat any amendment." Mr. Webster was chairman of the committee that dealt with this subject, and though the original committee report favored a two-thirds vote of each House,[1] yet in deference to the objections raised he himself moved to amend so as to require a majority of the Senate and two-thirds of the House of Representatives present and voting thereon.[2]

In connection with this provision for amending the constitution we ought to consider the possibility of adopting amendments in some other way. Of course the only other way would be by calling a constitutional convention. With this provision in the constitution would it be proper to call a constitutional convention either to amend the constitution or to draw up a new constitution?

[1] *Journal of the Convention*, 1820, p. 124.
[2] *Ibid.*, p. 404.

Both the Convention of 1820 and that of 1853 were called for the purpose of *revising or altering* the Constitution. The Convention of 1820 followed this mandate and submitted amendments only. The Convention of 1853 submitted amendments and also proposed what was practically a new constitution. Of course in 1820 there was no provision for amendment in the Constitution, that clause not coming into effect until the Convention had adjourned and the article submitted by it had been adopted by the people.

In 1833 the judges were asked their opinion, first, whether if the legislature submitted to the people the question of calling a convention for revising or altering the constitution in any specified parts of the same and the people voted favorably, the convention could propose amendments in other parts of the constitution not so specified; and, second, whether any specific or particular amendment could be made to the constitution in any other manner than that prescribed in the ninth article of the amendments. The judges answered to the first question that "considering that the constitution has vested no authority in the legislature, in its ordinary action, to provide by law for submitting to the people the expediency of calling a convention of delegates, for the purpose of revising or altering the constitution of the commonwealth, it is difficult to give an opinion upon the question, what would be the power of such a convention, if called. If, however, the people should, by the terms of their vote, decide to call a convention of delegates to consider the expediency of altering the constitution in some particular part thereof, we are of opinion that such delegates would derive their whole authority and commission from such vote; and, upon the general principles governing the delegation of power and authority, they would have no right, under such vote, to act upon and propose amendments in other parts of the constitution not so specified."[1] And on the second question, that "under and pursuant to the existing constitution, there is no authority given by any reasonable construction or necessary implication, by which any specific and particular amendment or amendments of the constitution can be made, in any other manner than that prescribed in the ninth article of the amendments adopted in 1820. Considering that previous to 1820 no mode was provided by the constitution for its own amendment, that no other power for that purpose, than in the mode alluded to, is anywhere given in the constitution, by implication or otherwise, and that the mode thereby provided appears manifestly to have been carefully considered, and the power of altering the constitution thereby conferred to have been cautiously restrained and guarded, we think a strong implication arises against the existence of any other power, under the constitution, for the same purposes."[2]

Light is also given us in relation to this matter by the words of Mr. Webster in offering the resolution for amending the constitution in the Convention of 1820 where he suggests that after the amendments adopted by the Convention of 1820 there was slight chance of a demand arising for any great changes. "No revision of its general principles would be necessary and the alterations which should be called for by a change of circumstances would be limited and specific. It was therefore the opinion of the committee that no provision for a revision of the whole constitution was expedient and the only question was in what manner it should be provided that particular amendments might be obtained. It was a natural course and conformable to analogy and prece-

[1] 6 Cushing (*Mass.*), 574–575.
[2] *Ibid.*, p. 574.

dent in some degree that every proposition for amendment should originate in the legislature under certain guards and be sent out to the people." [1]

And in the address issued by the Convention to the people the statement is made, among other things, that "it may be necessary that specific amendments of the constitution should hereafter be made. The preparatory measures in assembling a convention, and the necessary expense of such an assembly, are obstacles of some magnitude, to obtaining amendments through such means; . . . We believe that the constitution will be sufficiently guarded from inexpedient alterations, while all those which are found to be necessary, will be duly considered and may be obtained with comparatively small expense." [2]

There is also an opinion of the judges in Rhode Island as to calling a convention to frame a new constitution and the judges answered that it could not be done as the Constitution had a provision for amendment.[3]

From the above quotations and authorities we can arrive at fairly definite conclusions in relation to this complicated subject. We note that in the Massachusetts case the opinion was on the question of calling a convention to make specific amendments, while in the Rhode Island case it was as to calling a convention to draw up a new constitution. The language above quoted as used in the Convention of 1820 also shows that the delegates had in mind not a general revision of the constitution but merely the adoption of specific amendments. Thus it would be quite natural and expected that while the legislature might submit the proposition for calling a convention to frame a new constitution or to revise the old one in indefinite and undetermined re-

[1] *Journal of the Convention*, 1820, p. 413.

[2] *Ibid.*, p. 631. [3] 14 *Rhode Island*, 649.

spects yet where the constitution provides a definite method for the adoption of specific amendments no such amendments can be adopted in any other way. This power would not be included under a general grant of legislative power. The power to propose amendments to the constitution is not a legislative power, and therefore does not exist unless provided for in the constitution. Yet it seems to be granted, except in the Rhode Island case, that the legislature has power to call a convention unless there be express prohibition in the constitution. This is established by long usage and also by general legislative power extending to all subjects not prohibited by their own or the federal constitution.[1]

Any one who desired to obtain an excellent and exhaustive discussion of this whole subject should consult Jameson's standard work on Constitutional Conventions. In dealing with the question of a convention's exceeding its powers he is also illuminating. A convention would seem to derive its powers from the vote adopted by the people in calling it. Yet the majority of the delegates in 1853, though called only to alter or revise the Constitution, proceeded to submit a new constitution. They exceeded their powers, but having the votes nothing seemed to stand in their way. What the Courts would have said was left undetermined as the people took the decision into their own hands by rejecting the work of this Convention when it was referred to them. The delegates who framed the Constitution of the United States in a similar manner may also have exceeded the authority given them, but the people of the several States in that case ratified their work.

[1] Jameson, *Treatise on Constitutional Conventions*, sec. 574, *h*.

# CHAPTER IV

## THE CONSTITUTIONAL CONVENTION OF 1853

FOUR amendments to the Constitution were adopted between the Convention of 1820 and that of 1853. They related to the change in the political year, to public worship, to the number of, and the method of electing, members of the House, Senate and Council, and to the abolition of a freehold or any other estate as a qualification for holding a seat in the General Court or the Executive Council.

In 1851 a majority of the people voted against an Act submitted to them by the Legislature providing for the calling of a constitutional convention. In the following year the question was again submitted, and they voted favorably on it.

The Convention met on the 4th of May, 1853, at the State House in Boston. Nathaniel P. Banks, Jr., was chosen President. The Convention adjourned on the first of August after finishing its work, providing for the submission of the same to the people, and appointing a committee to meet and count the votes. The new constitution submitted by the Convention was rejected by the people. The proceedings of the Convention were of so much importance, however, its reasons for submitting the various propositions, the causes of rejection by the people, and the discussions on the various points at issue are so interesting, are so illuminating, that it is well worth while entering into a consideration of its history. Though there were many good propositions in the Constitution submitted there were also bad ones, and in spite of the precept *de mortuis nil nisi bonum* I feel at liberty to criticize that part of the work.

## PERSONNEL AND WORK OF THE CONVENTION

There was much opposition in the Convention to the adoption of various propositions, but the Whig party as a whole was discredited, and politics played a great part in the proceedings as well as in the initial calling of the Convention. Under the call for the Convention, each town and city was to elect as many delegates as it had representatives in the General Court. They were called together just as they had been in 1820, for the purpose of revising or altering the Constitution of government of the Commonwealth.[1]

Henry Wilson, who was later Senator from Massachusetts and Vice-President of the United States, John Davis, who had been Governor and Senator, Henry L. Dawes, who was also afterwards Senator, Charles Sumner, who was then Senator, Messrs. Morton, Briggs and Boutwell, all of whom had been Governors of Massachusetts, and Messrs. Banks and Butler, who were destined to be Governors, were all members of this Convention, as were also such able attorneys as Mr. Choate, who had been Senator, Mr. Bartlett, of Boston, and many other distinguished men.

Eight distinct propositions were submitted to the people.

The first proposition was a new constitution.
The second related to habeas corpus.
The third related to the rights of juries.
The fourth related to claims against the Commonwealth.
The fifth related to imprisonment for debt.
The sixth related to sectarian schools.
The seventh related to the creation of corporations.
The eighth related to the formation of banks and requiring security for bank bills.

[1] As to the legality of the action taken by this Convention, see *above*, pp. 47–50.

The most important proposals and alterations were placed in the new constitution. There was much opposition to submitting any questions to be voted on as single propositions. Certainly if any were to be submitted they should all have been submitted as one constitution or else as separate propositions and not some jumbled together in a new constitution and others left to the people as separate amendments, some of which could have been passed as Legislative acts.

To return, however, to proposition number one — the new constitution. It is an enlightening document but some of its provisions were very unscientific, to say the least. The whole thing was a jumble and a series of political compromises. Let me touch on a few of the important changes proposed.

## Changes Proposed in the Rejected "New Constitution" of 1853

Sessions of the General Court were to be limited to one hundred days. Forty senatorial districts were provided for to take the place of county representation. The property qualification for the Governor and Lieutenant-Governor was abolished. Town representation for the House of Representatives was still maintained but altered to some degree. A Council of eight districts was provided for. The direct election by the people of Attorney-General,[1] Treasurer, Auditor, and Secretary[2] was established. Property qualification for voting was abolished.

And then followed provisions which probably led to the defeat of the whole constitution, but which were apparently

[1] Appointed by the Governor under the Constitution. Chap. II, § I, Art. IX.

[2] Chosen by the Legislature under the Constitution. Chap. II, § IV Art. I. *Acts of 1849*, Chap. 56. *Acts of 1908*, Chap. 597.

put in the same instrument instead of being left as separate amendments because the supporters of the doctrines thought that by being included with so many good things they would have a better chance of adoption than if left to stand on their own merits. These clauses provided not only for the election of sheriffs,[1] district attorneys, clerks of court, etc., all of which offices have since quite properly become elective, but also for the election of probate judges[1] and for the appointment of judges of the Supreme Court and the Court of Common Pleas for a term limited to ten years. There was also a provision for voting every twenty years on the question of holding a constitutional convention. This proposition was mandatory, and gave the people no choice as to whether or not they wanted to vote on the question.

The best among these various propositions were adopted later as separate amendments to the Constitution. For instance, in 1855, amendments were accepted providing for eight Councillors to be chosen by districts; for election by the people of the Secretary, Treasurer, Auditor, and Attorney-General; for the election of sheriffs, registers of probate, clerks of court, and district attorneys. In 1857 a change in the method of election of the House of Representatives was adopted, and instead of continuing the system of town representation, provision was made for a House of Representatives of two hundred and forty members apportioned to the several counties as equally as possible, according to the number of voters. In the same year, too, forty senatorial districts were provided for, one senator to come from each district, and each district to contain as nearly as possible an equal number of voters.

The third amendment of the Constitution, adopted in 1820, had done away with all the property qualifications for

[1] See note 1, page 53.

voting except payment of a state and county tax. In 1891 even this tax requirement was done away with as had been suggested in this proposed constitution of 1853, so that from 1891 on not even payment of a poll tax was required as a condition for voting. The property qualification for Governor and Lieutenant-Governor was abolished by an amendment passed in 1892.

## Where the Proposed Constitution of 1853 was at Fault

I have now spoken of the most important changes provided for in this proposed constitution. There was a great deal of brilliant discussion and much illuminating debate in the convention itself, and afterwards numerous speeches were made and letters written, some under assumed and sonorous names, in relation to the document. Eminent Whigs and Democrats assailed the document, aiming their shafts particularly at the disproportionate representation provided for in the House of Representatives, and the change of method in judicial tenure.

### (*a*) *In the Apportionment of Representatives*

The apportionment of representatives was unfair. For instance, the town of Hingham, with 3,962 inhabitants, was to have one representative and the town of Chesterfield, with 1,009 inhabitants, was also to have one. According to Governor Morton, thirty towns with a population of 16,292 were entitled to thirty representatives, while New Bedford, with 16,441 inhabitants, was given only five representatives. Naturally the cities would not allow such an apportionment to be thrust down their throats.

### (b) *In Limiting the Tenure of Judges*

The proposal to have a limited tenure for judges was excoriated by many distinguished men. The arguments against it were well stated. Let me quote the words of G. S. Hillard, who wrote under the name of Silas Standfast. In speaking of the proposed election of probate judges he says:

> A judge of probate stands in relations to the community which demand, above all things else, honesty, firmness, and impartiality. He must be above suspicion in these respects. He is constantly deciding questions of property; and the purse-vein of our people beats sensitively. He has to pass upon matters where family feeling is involved, — to lay his hand upon chords which run back to the core of the heart. At present, — holding his office upon the tenure of good behavior, — directly responsible only to the Legislature, who may remove or impeach him, — we can rely upon the best exercise of his best faculties. The judge of probate is now, to borrow the language of the Constitution, "as free, impartial, and independent, as the lot of humanity will admit." But elect him for three years, make him responsible to a political party and a political press, and it cannot be so.[1]

As the the proposed change in tenure of Judges of the Supreme Court and Court of Common Pleas from life to a term of ten years, he is still more explicit and I wish to quote him more at length:

> The judge is, first, a man; second, a lawyer; and, third, a judge. The framers of our admirable Constitution proposed to themselves two objects in regard to the Judiciary: First, to get the best possible judges; and, second, to secure afterwards the best exercise of their best judicial faculties. The proposed change will do neither. It will give us judges inferior to those we have always had, and will expose them to dangerous influences and temptations heretofore unknown in Massachusetts.
>
> What is the first great quality in a judge? Beyond all question, INDEPENDENCE. He may be learned, wise, and conscientious; but if

[1] *Discussions on the Constitution proposed to the people of Massachusetts by The Convention of 1853*, p. 141.

he be not independent, if he have not the courage which rests upon independence, there is not the least security that his good qualities will move in the right direction. This is the guardian virtue, which stands at the gate and keeps watch over the rest. Now, let the judge know and feel that the Governor, at the end of ten years, may or may not reappoint him; suppose him also to be a man of little property, and dependent for the just support of his family upon his income, — do you imagine that he will be perfectly independent, that no shadow of apprehension, no touch of favor, will ever pass over his mind? . . .

Judges are cut out of the same cloth as other men, and I know enough of human nature to know that *all* men should pray fervently to be delivered from temptation. . . .

It is a stern fact, from which there is no escaping, *that he who controls a man's bread exerts, sensibly or insensibly, more or less control over his thoughts and his will.* I do not mean to say, that, come what will, we shall have base, venal, and corrupt judges in Massachusetts, or that their sycophancy and subserviency will be palpable, glaring, monstrous; but I *do* say, that the lofty and eminent excellence which we have had in that department will no longer be there; and that we must hereafter be content to associate with our ideas of a judge, a less conspicuous merit, and a less distinguished ability, than we now rest upon for the protection of our persons, our property, and our characters, — in short, all that is worth protecting or living for.

As a man thinketh in his heart, says the wise man, so is he. This saying, applicable in so many ways, applies also to the case of judges. At present, no man, however dissatisfied he may be with the decisions of the court, can say, or have reason to think, that the judges have been moved by anything but their convictions; but let them be in a position to give color to the charge of being actuated by foreign influences, and especially political biases, and discontent will be sure to vent itself in that way. You know how many of the cases that come before our courts have more or less of a political aspect, especially constitutional cases, and you also know that many lawyers are vehement politicians; but perhaps you do not know what I can tell you, that there are *some* lawyers who cannot conceive it to be consistent with the scheme of Divine Providence in the government of this world, that *they* should ever be mistaken. Therefore, when the court decides against *them*, they feel as if chaos were come again, — that suns will cease to rise, and stars refuse to shine. Now would you like to see such a state of things in Massachusetts, as that a lawyer-politician might ventilate

[1] *Discussions on the Constitution proposed to the people of Massachusetts by The Convention of 1853*, p. 152.

his wrath, after an adverse decision, in words like these, muttered in the bar, but not inaudible: "You think it a fine thing to sit up there on the bench and make law to suit your own politics; but your course will soon be run. Your ten years will be out next year, and we will pitch you overboard with as little ceremony as you pitch overboard a law that does not suit you, and put a man in your place who will have some sympathy with the people, and respect their wishes a little more than such an old fogie as you." . . . And just so here, the Judiciary stands between the *government* and the *individual*, and it ought to stand there; but then the *government* here is the *people;* and we want a Judiciary strong enough *to protect the individual against the people, in case the people should be wrong.* We want a judge who will *not* fear a political party or a political press. We insist that every criminal, however odious his crime may be have been, should have a *fair* and *dispassionate* trial. We claim and need a Judiciary strong enough to protect a trembling culprit against popular violence and political persecution. We insist, when the constitutionality of a law is before the court, that no judge should feel that his chance of reappointment may be affected by his decision. We claim to have political offenders tried as impartially, — with as much freedom from executive influence, — as John Marshall tried Aaron Burr. Does any man say that John Marshall would have tried Aaron Burr in the same way, had the tenure of the Judges of the Supreme Court been for ten years? I reply, that, with such a provision in the Constitution of the United States, you would never have had John Marshall, or any man like him, on the bench.

The Judiciary of Massachusetts is one of the brightest jewels in her honored crown; we do not perceive all its lustre, because it is worn upon our own brow. But go to Arkansas, to Wisconsin, to Georgia, and ask there what is the authority of the Massachusetts Reports, and you would be enlightened on this subject. Your heart would swell with honorable pride at the respect paid, in those distant States, to the decisions of *our* Judges, whom the new Constitution insults by virtually pronouncing them unfit to appoint their own clerks! Such influence as we exert, through our courts, is one of the purest and highest that man can have over man. It has no alloy of passion or prejudice; it is the calm supremacy of truth, reason and conscience. Are we to renounce this? Are we to throw it away in pure wantonness? I trow not. The people have been taken by surprise upon this question of the Judiciary. They will give their answer at the polls.[1]

[1] *Discussions on the Constitution proposed to the people of Massachusetts by The Convention, of 1853*, pp. 153-155.

## Conclusion

The question was decisively answered at the polls. The hope of those who thought to get through some of these amendments by holding out as a bait to the people other things in the Constitution which they wanted, were doomed to disappointment. The proposed Constitution and all the propositions submitted therewith, good and bad, were one and all voted down. Massachusetts continues, therefore, under her original Constitution adopted in 1780. It has an efficient method of amendment. This is much less expensive than calling delegates together in convention and more is apt to be accomplished for the people by leaving distinct and separate questions to them than by jumbling so many together in one document as was done in 1853. If separate amendments are submitted the people can vote for the ones they want and against the ones they do not want. They cannot be duped now any more than they could be in 1853 by party cliques and political coalitions into accepting things they do not want for the sake of getting other things which they do want. They thought that by waiting they could obtain what they desired without taking bitter pills along with it, and the fact that almost immediately separate amendments were adopted by the Legislature and sent to the voters covering the parts of the Constitution where it was known a change was desired, shows that they were right.

# CHAPTER V

## THE GENERAL COURT

THE Constitution of 1780 provided that the legislative body of the Commonwealth should be styled the General Court of Massachusetts. This is a name that is unusual and distinctive because in most States, the two legislative bodies are commonly called the Legislature. The name arose from the fact that originally the body heard judicial questions and was the final court to which the people could go on general matters, both legal and legislative. Yet it is commonly known as the Legislature, even by people in Massachusetts. I remember once when Dr. Everett was to deliver an historical address at the Old South Church, one of the ushers, a college graduate and presumably well-informed citizen, came up and asked him who the men were for whom certain seats were reserved, and when the Doctor told him they were for the General Court he remarked that he thought they were for the Legislature.

### ORIGINAL PROVISIONS

As has been said, the first General Court under the Constitution consisted of two hundred members.[1] It was not many years before the membership of the House of Representatives alone exceeded that figure and often rose to over four hundred, until in the year 1857 an amendment to the Constitution was adopted providing that the House of Representatives should consist of two hundred and forty

[1] See *above*, p. 27.

members.[1] The Senate was at first composed of forty men elected as councillors and senators, nine persons being annually chosen from this number by joint ballot of the Senate and House of Representatives to act as councillors. This vacated their seats in the Senate and left an upper branch of only thirty-one. As a seat in that body was more desirable, being more influential than a seat in the Council, men frequently refused to allow themselves to be elected into the Council.

## Changes by Various Constitutional Amendments

At first there had been a great deal of discussion as to whether there should be a bi-cameral legislature or not,[2] and we have seen how the men advocating this system prevailed over those who favored a single chamber. The plan of government was modeled so that the Senate or upper branch should represent property, and the House, persons. Accordingly, it was provided that the General Court in assigning the number of senators to be elected by each district should govern themselves by the proportion of taxes paid by the district. In 1840, provision was made for separating the election of councillors and senators.[3] Forty senators were to be chosen from the former districts and nine councillors were to be chosen by joint ballot from the people at large. This amendment also did away with the property qualification as a condition for holding a seat in either branch of the General Court or in the Executive Council, but provision is still retained in the Constitution that to be a member of the Senate or the Governor's Council one must have been an

[1] *Constitution of Massachusetts*, Article of Amendment XXI.

[2] See *above*, p. 22, and note.

[3] *Constitution of Massachusetts*, Article of Amendment XIII.

inhabitant of the Commonwealth for at least five years immediately preceding his election. A member of the House must have been an inhabitant of the district from which he is chosen one year next preceding his election. Senators, also, must be inhabitants of their district at the time of election and both they and representatives cease to represent their districts when they cease to be inhabitants of the Commonwealth.

Another amendment in 1855[1] made provision for the present mode of electing councillors by establishing that the Commonwealth be divided into eight districts, with one councillor elected from each district by the voters and not by the General Court as heretofore had been the custom. Two years later Amendment XXII was ratified, providing that the old senatorial districts should be abandoned and new districts laid out from time to time, each district to contain as nearly as possible, an equal number of legal voters. Representation, both in the House and in the Senate is, accordingly, now based on persons and not on property.

Originally, too, voters had to be possessed of a free-hold estate of the annual income of three pounds, or any estate of the value of sixty pounds. Article III of the Amendments did away with all but a poll tax qualification and even that was abolished by the thirty-second Article of the Amendments. Vacancies in the House and in the Senate are filled by the people from the districts, and the Governor and the Legislature have nothing to do with this matter as they have in the case of a vacancy in the office of Secretary of State, Attorney General or other State officer or a member of the Executive Council. Up to 1860, however, vacancies in the Senate were filled by the Legislature.[2] In that year an amendment was

[1] *Constitution of Massachusetts*, Article of Amendment XVI.
[2] *Ibid.*, Chap. I, § 2, Art. IV.

ratified providing that all vacancies in that body be filled by election by the people of the unrepresented districts upon the order of a majority of the senators elected.[1]

Provisions that sixteen senators should constitute a quorum and not less than sixty members of the House, were done away with by an amendment passed in 1891, which substituted a majority of the members in each House.[2]

## Annual Elections and Sessions

The Legislature of Massachusetts has always met every year and been elected every year. Several other States of the Union have yearly sessions of their Legislatures but Massachusetts is the only one left having both yearly sessions and yearly elections. To be sure, a change has been agitated and proposed articles of amendment adopted by the Legislatures of 1895 and 1896 were submitted to the people, providing for biennial elections of State officers, and providing for biennial elections of members of the General Court. Both proposals were rejected.

The General Court was given power to establish courts,[3] to pass laws not repugnant to the Constitution, to name and style or pass laws for naming and styling all civil officers whose election or appointment had not been provided for in the Constitution. It was also given power to impose proportional and reasonable assessments, rates and taxes, and to impose reasonable duties and excises upon any produce, goods, wares, merchandise and commodities, and was required to provide for a valuation of estates at least once in every ten years.[4] The question of taxation and the con-

[1] Article of Amendment XXIV.
[2] *Ibid.*, XXXIII.
[3] *Constitution of Massachusetts*, Chap. I, § I, Art. III.
[4] *Ibid.*, Chap. I, § I, Art. IV. Article of Amendment XLIV.

struction of these clauses is too exhaustive a subject to be treated by me in this little outline. There are plenty of valuable books and court decisions on this most important subject.

### Power to Grant City Charters

The second article of amendment gave to the General Court power to charter cities, provided that the town contained twelve thousand inhabitants and a majority of them voted for incorporation as a city. Strange to say, up to this time no city had existed in Massachusetts. It was not until two years later, in 1822, that Boston became a city and she was the first one in Massachusetts. Colonial Governors granted charters in many of the colonies but not in Massachusetts. The first city in this country to receive a charter was New York in 1686.[1]

### Direct Legislation

It is a far cry from 1686 to 1913 and from the second amendment to the forty-second, but in the sequence of events it is not such a stretch as the one we noted between the referendum of the Plymouth Colony and that same question today.[2]

The forty-second amendment, ratified in 1913, provides that the General Court may refer to the people for their rejection or approval at the polls any act or resolve or any part or parts thereof. This amendment was adopted as the judges had given an opinion that a State-wide referendum would be unconstitutional.[3] For many years the use of the referendum had been agitated in the various States of the Union. Some States had adopted it and also gone further

[1] W. B. Munro, *Government of American Cities*, p. 2.

[2] See *above*, pp. 4, 5.

[3] 160 *Massachusetts*, 586.

and adopted the initiative which allows the people on petition of a certain number of voters to initiate a law as well as to have it submitted to them after its passage through the Legislature. Massachusetts held out for a long time and when she did adopt the principle she did not adopt the compulsory referendum but only empowered the General Court to attach a referendum clause to such measures as it might see fit. Up to this time the Legislature had no power to do this to the extent of a State-wide referendum as the case referred to shows.

### Amendments to Permit the Use of Voting Machines

When voting machines were invented there was much discussion as to the legality of using them in Massachusetts, it being contended that the Constitution contemplated the marking of ballots by each individual with his own hand, and not by mechanical device. Indeed, the Constitution provides specifically that every member of the House shall be chosen by written votes.[1] The question was referred to the Judges of the Supreme Court for an opinion and the majority decided that the use of voting machines would be constitutional.[2] This question was afterwards put beyond range of doubt by an amendment to the Constitution, adopted in 1911, specifically providing that voting machines might be used.[3]

### Constitutional Privileges of Senate and House

The Senate and House are both made judges of the qualifications of their own members.[4] Each body, in other words,

[1] *Constitution of Massachusetts*, Chap. I, § III, Art. III.

[2] 178 *Massachusetts*, 605. [3] Article of Amendment XXXVIII.

[4] *Constitution of Massachusetts*, Chap. I, § II, Art. IV, and Chap. I, § III, Art. X, respectively.

can eject one of its members for any cause, or apparently for no assigned cause. It is customary to have a committee appointed and regular hearings given, though this is not required. The Senate, the House, and the Governor and Council have authority to punish by imprisonment every person not a member who shall be guilty of disrespect by disorderly or contemptuous behavior in its presence or who shall threaten harm to the body or estate of its members for anything said or done in the sitting or who shall assault any of them or assault or arrest any witness or other person ordered to attend them, while going or returning, or who shall rescue any person arrested by their order, but no imprisonment shall exceed thirty days.[1] No member of the House can be arrested while he is attending the Assembly or going to or returning from the same.

## The Impeachment Power

In connection with the right of the House and Senate to oust their own members, we should distinguish this from the power of impeachment. Such impeachments are brought by the House of Representatives, and are tried before the Senate. Any officer of the Commonwealth is liable to impeachment for misconduct and mal-administration in office.[2] A member of the House or Senate is probably not such an officer of the Commonwealth and indeed whether legislators are ever subject to impeachment in this country is a disputed question. United States Senators have been held not to be civil officers of the United States as they are delegated by the States.[3] Many interesting questions have

[1] *Constitution of Massachusetts*, Chap. I, § III, Arts. X, XI.

[2] *Ibid.*, Chap. I, § II, Art. VIII, and *Revised Laws of Massachusetts*, Chap. 6, § 3, providing that the Governor and Council may remove the State Treasurer under certain circumstances.

[3] Finley and Sanderson, *American Executive and Executive Methods*, p. 60.

arisen in connection with impeachment proceedings. When an accusation is formally presented the accused is said to be impeached. If that accusation is sustained and judgment pronounced, the accused is convicted on impeachment. The Constitution of New York State is peculiar in this matter, Article IV, section 6 providing that "in case of the impeachment of the Governor," . . . etc., "the powers and duties of the office shall devolve upon the Lieutenant-Governor . . ."

When the charges against Governor Sulzer were laid before the Senate by the duly appointed Committee of the Assembly, the question arose whether or not the Governor was, under the Constitution, thereby superseded in office by the Lieutenant-Governor. Under the Constitution of the United States the chief Executive would not be ousted until convicted on impeachment. We had an example of this when Andrew Johnson was impeached but not convicted. He remained President during his trial. In Massachusetts the same rule would apply, but under the special wording of the New York Constitution it was held that as soon as the Assembly adopts and presents to the Senate its accusation, the Governor ceases to act as such and may resume the functions of Governor only when and if acquitted.

### Impeachment in Massachusetts

There have been several cases of impeachment in Massachusetts. The course of proceeding is to file a petition at the State House for impeachment. Then a special committee of the House is appointed to act thereon or the matter may be sent to one of the regular committees. If the committee reports in favor of impeachment it must be because of alleged misconduct or mal-administration in office. The report being adopted by the House, a committee is then appointed to go to the Bar of the Senate and in the name of the House to impeach and exhibit articles of impeachment. The House appoints managers to conduct the trial and the Senate is duly sworn and sits as a court to hear the evidence. The Constitution provides that when they render judgment it shall not extend further than removal from office and disqualification from holding office in the Commonwealth. A convicted official, however, is also liable to indictment, trial and punishment, according to the laws of the land.

The first case that arose in Massachusetts seems to have been that of William Greenleaf, Sheriff of Worcester County. The proceedings were held in Faneuil Hall on the charge that the accused had collected money and kept it illegally. The Sheriff was found guilty and removed from office. That was in 1788. In 1794 a justice of the peace, William Hunt, was impeached, and the session was again held in Faneuil Hall. In 1800 and in 1807, two other justices of the peace were impeached, the judgment in the second case being "not guilty." In 1821 James Prescott, Judge of the Middlesex Probate Court, was impeached, convicted and removed from office.

In England, all subjects, whether officials or not, are liable to impeachment. Not so in Massachusetts, as we have seen, where the Constitution limits it to officers of the Commonwealth. Originally, impeachment was a criminal proceeding. In some jurisdictions it is even now held that the offense must be an indictable one. The United States Senate, however, has convicted upon impeachment even though the offense was not indictable at common law or under the Federal statutes. In Pennsylvania a judge was once impeached for preventing an associate from delivering an opinion. It is also interesting to consider what would happen in Massachusetts if an official should resign after being impeached. The trial of ex-Secretary Belknap proceeded before the United States Senate after he had resigned. The question is not absolutely settled, yet a man after resignation ceases to be a civil officer and becomes a private citizen.

### The Originating of "Money Bills"

The House of Representatives being the popular branch as it represented persons and not property, the Constitution of 1780 provided that all money bills should originate there,[1] the Senate having the right, however, to propose or concur with amendments as on other bills. The determination of just what this expression "money bills" meant has given rise to considerable speculation. In Massachusetts it has been decided that the words are limited to bills transferring money or property from the people to the State. In other words it includes only bills for raising revenue. A bill appropriating money from the Treasury of the Commonwealth is not a "money bill." An elaborate opinion covering this whole subject in great detail and tracing the history of the question from the early days of the English Parliament was delivered by the Massachusetts Supreme Judicial Court in 1878, in answer to questions from the Senate and House of Representatives.[2]

### Adjournments

Both the House and the Senate have the right to adjourn for a period not exceeding two days. If they want to adjourn for a longer time or wish to prorogue, they must have the consent of the Governor and Council.[3] This power of the

[1] *Constitution of Massachusetts*, Chap. I, § III, Art. VII.

[2] 126 *Massachusetts*, 557. [3] Chap. I, § II, Art. VI and § III, Art. VIII.

Legislature to adjourn itself was one of the matters in dispute, it will be remembered, in the provincial days,— one of the things that led to the passage of the explanatory charter in 1726, and the above provision was evidently copied into the Constitution directly from the power granted there.[1]

## Incompatible Offices

Before closing this chapter on the General Court we should note various clauses in the Constitution providing against holding incompatible offices. For instance, no Judge of the Supreme Judicial Court, or Judge of Probate, Secretary, Attorney-General or Treasurer of the Commonwealth, Sheriff, Clerk of the House, Register of Probate, Register of Deeds or Clerk of the Supreme Court can sit in the Senate or House of Representatives. In early days this prohibition extended also to the president, a professor or an instructor in Harvard College, but this disability was removed in 1877.[2] If a member of the Massachusetts Senate or House accept one of the above offices, he thereby impliedly resigns his seat in the Legislature. Also if a judge of the Supreme or Probate Court accept a seat in the Council he thereby ceases to be a judge and if a member of the Council accepts a place on the Supreme bench or the Probate Court bench he thereby vacates his seat in the Council.[3] The same article also provides that no one shall hold more than one of the following offices, namely, "Judge of Probate, Sheriff, Register of Probate, or Register of Deeds; and never more than any two offices, which are to be held by appointment of the Governor, or the Governor and Council, or the Senate, or the House of Representatives, or by the

[1] See *above*, p. 14. [2] Article of Amendment XXVII.

[3] *Constitution of Massachusetts*, Chap. VI, Art. II.

election of the people of the State at large, or of the people of any county, military offices and the offices of justices of the peace excepted."

An amendment to the Constitution[1] provides that "no judge of any court of this commonwealth (except the court of sessions), and no person holding any office under the authority of the United States (postmasters excepted), shall at the same time hold the office of governor, lieutenant-governor, or councillor, or have a seat in the senate or house of representatives of this commonwealth; and no judge of any court in this commonwealth (except the court of sessions), nor the attorney-general, solicitor-general, county-attorney, clerk of any court, sheriff, treasurer and receiver-general, register of probate, nor register of deeds, shall continue to hold his said office after being elected a member of the Congress of the United States and accepting that trust, but the acceptance of such trust by any of the officers aforesaid shall be deemed and taken to be a resignation of his said office."

These articles in the Constitution have been brought before the Supreme Court of Massachusetts for explanation and interpretation. The House of Representatives once asked the judges whether by Article VIII of the Amendments a special justice of the district, police or municipal court vacated his office by accepting a seat in the House of Representatives. The judges refused to answer the question because, they said: "The question now referred to us does not regard the construction or effect of any statute, or of any contract with the Commonwealth, or any matter which can be affected by legislation. It depends upon a provision of the Constitution which so far as it applies, operates by its own force. The question does not purport to relate to the election or qualifications of a member of the House of Repre-

[1] Article of Amendment VIII.

sentatives. But the question is whether a certain judicial officer by accepting a seat in the House, vacates his judicial office. This appears to us to be not a legislative but a judicial question which cannot be definitely or justly decided without trial and argument."[1]

But in another case where the question came before them in a judicial manner in the nature of *quo warranto* proceedings, they held that a judge vacated his office by acceptance of a seat in the House of Representatives and that a special justice of a police court was such a judge as is referred to in the Constitution, saying: "If he did not lawfully hold a seat in the House he could be unseated only by the House itself, which is by the Constitution the final judge of the elections, returns and qualifications of its own members (Constitution of Massachusetts, c. 1, § 3, art. 10). But if he unlawfully holds a judicial office, this proceeding by information in behalf of the Commonwealth is the proper process to oust him from the office which he occupies *de facto*, but to which he has no legal right."[2] Of course there is nothing to make the holder of one of these offices ineligible for another, but he must resign one before accepting the other. Thus a judge of probate has been held by the House of Representatives eligible to take his seat in the House if he resigned his judicial office after election.[3]

[1] 122 *Massachusetts*, 603. See also p. 84 *below*.

[2] 123 *Massachusetts*, 529.

[3] Case of Sullivan, *Massachusetts Election Cases* (ed. 1853) p. 39.

# CHAPTER VI

## THE GOVERNOR

THE Governor and the other State officers of Massachusetts are elected for terms of one year. The Governor must have been an inhabitant of the Commonwealth for the seven preceding years. Though elected annually it is generally understood and may be called an unwritten rule that a Governor, if his administration proves satisfactory, is entitled to three terms. In former times he was often re-elected for more than three terms. Thus we find that John Hancock, the first Governor under the Constitution, held the office first for five years and later for six. John Davis and Marcus Morton were also twice Governor. But in neither case did their terms exceed three years at one time. John Davis retired from the Governorship on becoming Senator and on leaving the Senate became Governor again. Governor Morton was elected to his first term by the narrowest plurality ever given. He defeated Edward Everett for a fourth term by one vote. I wonder if they allowed recounts in those days! Governor John A. Andrew was the last chief Executive to have a term of over three years.

Originally, a majority vote was required to elect both Governor and Lieutenant-Governor, and if no candidate received a majority vote the election was thrown into the Legislature. If no one received a majority vote for Governor the vote in the Legislature was not by joint ballot, but the House chose two out of the highest four names and the Senate chose the Chief Executive from them.[1] In 1855 a

[1] *Constitution of Massachusetts*, Chap. II, § I, Art. III.

plurality vote was provided for by amendment to the Constitution. So today the election of a Governor or Lieutenant-Governor is never thrown into the Legislature. If a vacancy is caused by the death of the Governor or by his absence or for any other reason, the Lieutenant-Governor succeeds; and if, for similar reasons, the Lieutenant-Governor is unable to serve "the Council or a majority thereof" becomes Chief Executive.[1]

## The Governor's Title

The Constitution of Massachusetts provides that the title of the Governor shall be "His Excellency." This title arose in the provincial days. It was first used in 1699, when Governor Coote, Lord Bellomont, was Governor. As he was a lord it was thought proper to call him "Your Excellency." None of his predecessors were honored with any such title and his successors retained it only up to 1742, when an order from the King forbade its further use.[2] To the framers of the Constitution, then, the title was familiar and they thought proper to dignify the chief executive with it.

## Nomination of Candidates

At first in the State as in the nation party government was unknown. Hancock, Samuel Adams and Bowdoin were elected because of their standing in the community and their personal following. Before the Revolution, however, the names Whig and Tory were of course in use. Opposition to the Crown government gave birth to the party of liberation. Caucuses were held to discuss candidates for office. Such meetings had been held even in the days of Israel for the purpose of choosing judges. The word "caucus" is

[1] *Constitution of Massachusetts*, Chap. II, § III, Art. VI.
[2] Hutchinson, *History of Massachusetts*, Vol. III, p. 312.

said to have arisen from meetings held in the north end of Boston attended by shipping men and caulkers.

In general, candidates were self-announced according to the English custom at the period. This was particularly the case in the Southern States. In the Northeast and middle colonies parlor caucuses prevailed. John Adams in his diary[1] gives us an insight into the caucus of the period:

> Boston, February. This day learned that the Caucus Club meets, at certain times, in the garret of Tom Dawes, the Adjutant of the Boston Regiment. He has a large house, and he has a moveable partition in his garret which he takes down, and the whole club meets in one room. There they smoke tobacco till you cannot see from one end of the garret to the other. There they drink flip, I suppose, and there they choose a moderator, who puts questions to the vote regularly; and selectmen, assessors, collectors, wardens, fire-wards, and representatives, are regularly chosen before they are chosen in the town.[2] Uncle Fairfield, Story, Ruddock, Adams, Cooper, and a *rudis indigestaque moles* of others are members. They send committees to wait on the merchant's club, and to propose and join in the choice of men and measures. Captain Cunningham says, they have often solicited him to go to these caucuses; they have assured him benefit in his business, etc."

That the North End caucus did not limit itself strictly to nomination of candidates is shown by the vote it passed leading to the Boston Tea Party.[3]

[1] John Adams, *Works* (edition of 1850–1856) II, p. 144.

[2] Gordon assigns a very early date for this practice. He says, "More than fifty years ago," (from 1774) "Mr. Samuel Adams' father and twenty others, one or two from the north end of the town, where all ship business is carried on, used to meet, make a caucus and lay their plan for introducing certain persons into places of trust and power. When they had settled it, they separated, and used each their particular influence within his own circle. He and his friends would furnish themselves with ballots, including the names of the parties fixed upon, which they distributed on the days of election. By acting in concert, together with a careful and extensive distribution of ballots, they generally carried the elections to their own mind. In like manner it was, that Mr. Samuel Adams first became a representative for Boston." *History of the American Revolution*, vol. 1, p. 365, note.

[3] Richard Frothingham, *Life and Times of Joseph Warren*, pp. 238–240.

### Development of Nominating Methods

Although Massachusetts took the lead in so many political events she was behind other States, and notably Pennsylvania, in the adoption of a system for nominating candidates. Men at first were put in nomination by letters to the newspapers signed "An Elector," "A Citizen," etc. The lack of party organization led to a multiplicity of candidates. Governors and Lieutenant-Governors during the early period after the adoption of the Constitution were nominated by a meeting of party voters of the State held at some principal city. As the travelling was difficult, few attended, and consequently the nominating power fell on the shoulders of a handful of people.

This was practically a caucus. The next development from that was the usurpation of power by the members of the Legislature. Under the Constitution the Legislature was empowered to elect the State officers other than Governor and Lieutenant-Governor, and in case of the failure of any candidate for these executive positions to obtain a clear majority, the Legislature made the choice, though by a different procedure. The legislators of both parties, accordingly, took into their hands the powers of a convention and held regular caucuses at the State House to nominate their party tickets. This system we find firmly established by 1800. As communication became easier, however, the people took over these matters themselves, clipping the legislators of their power, and the convention system, with delegates elected from different parts of the State, took the place of the legislative caucus. The Democrats adopted the State Convention by 1828, the Whigs by 1840.

This development of methods of nomination in the State followed almost chronologically the succession of steps in the development of nominating machinery in the nation. There we find the nominations of the two parties for President after Washington being made by caucus of the representatives in Congress. This method gradually came into disrepute and its doom was sealed by the Adams-Jackson-Clay and Crawford contest of 1824. Then arose the system of having State Legislatures nominate candidates for President and finally that plan was repudiated and the method of nomination by a national convention consisting of delegates from each State was adopted.[1]

Confidence in party government grew until it became almost a fetish. The issues engendered by the Civil War added tremendously to its vitality. Even today, though party ties are no longer felt to be so binding, an independent candidacy has little chance of success. If a man with the popularity, prestige and accomplishments of Theodore Roosevelt could not succeed in winning an election without the nomination of one of the two great parties, no one could do so. And Mr. Foss, who had been thrice Governor in Massachusetts, received as an independent candidate scarcely a tenth of his former vote. Nevertheless, a distinct public sentiment favored more independence in nomination than was supposed to exist under the system of convention nominations. Too much control was thought to rest in the hands of a few party bosses. It has been in recognition of this opinion that legislation providing for nomination of candidates by filing a petition signed by a certain number of voters and for a general primary has been adopted. The Western States were the first to experiment with the scheme. Massachusetts, after trying this system of direct primary nominations on a small scale in various municipalities, finally bowed to public opinion and in 1911 adopted

[1] F. W. Dallinger, *Nominations for Elective Office*, Chap. I.

this plan for all State offices. It is too early to tell whether or not it is better than the old plan of having delegates, pledged or unpledged, nominate in a convention. The party convention now meets merely to hear speeches and draw up a platform, and its functions are apt to be too perfunctory and monotonous to attract the ablest men.

Whether it is easier to get a nomination under the new system I have grave doubts. Whether the system is a fairer one, remains to be proved. It certainly gives an advantage to the candidate with the longest purse and that surely is not a recommendation. I have been a candidate for the Republican nomination under both systems, under the old for Lieutenant-Governor, then under the new for Governor. In each case the contest was a hard one. In each case I was successful in obtaining the party's nomination but I think I would have won it under either method.

## The Governor's Duties and Powers

The Governor is inaugurated in the Representative Chamber in presence of both branches of the Legislature and such guests as he invites. The Lieutenant-Governor and Council are then sworn in, and the Governor proceeds to read his inaugural message to the assembled company. He may send messages to the General Court at any time it is in session. It is not customary for him to appear in person and read these messages. They are carried from the executive office by a secretary who marches down the centre aisle of the chamber with the sergeant-at-arms and delivers the document to the clerk, who reads it.

The Governor and the Lieutenant-Governor and Council visit the various institutions of the State, the insane asylums hospitals, prisons, schools for the feeble-minded and for the blind. This is always an important if an unpleasant duty.

The duties of a Governor are manifold. He is the Commander-in-Chief of the militia and the State naval forces and can assemble them for the special safety and defence of the Commonwealth. He cannot march them out of the Commonwealth without their consent or the consent of the General Court except to take them to some other part of the State.[1] He can call the Council together from time to time in his discretion.[2] He has power with advice of the Council to adjourn or prorogue the General Court when in session to any time the House and Senate may desire,[3] to call it together sooner than the time to which it may have been adjourned or prorogued if the welfare of the Commonwealth requires, and may direct the session to be held at some other more convenient place if for any reason danger may arise to the health of members from meeting at the place at which they would have convened. In case of disagreement between the two Houses he may, with the advice of the Council, adjourn or prorogue them not exceeding ninety days.[4]

The Governor is given the appointment of all judicial officers,[5] but the appointment is subject to the consent of the Council and the nomination must be made seven days before appointment. He has the appointment of the adjutant-general[6] and could appoint the attorney-general, sheriffs and registers of probate until these officers were made elective. Judges hold office during good behavior and justices of the peace for seven years. Amendment IV provided that notaries instead of being elected should be appointed for a seven-year term. Judges can only be removed by impeachment or on address.[7] This was originally true of justices of the peace as well and after Amendment IV of notaries, but

[1] *Constitution of Massachusetts*, Chap. II, § I, Art. VII.

[2] *Ibid.*, Art. IV.

[3] *Ibid.*, Art. V.

[4] *Ibid.*, Art. VI.

[5] *Ibid.*, Art. IX.

[6] *Ibid.*, Art. X.

[7] See *above*, p. 32.

Amendment XXXVII provided that justices of the peace and notaries might be removed by the Governor and Council.

In the many attempts to gain for women the right to vote and to hold office the question has been agitated as to a woman's right to be appointed a justice or a notary. The opinion of the judges was asked in 1871 as to a woman's serving as a justice and they answered in the negative because at the time the Constitution was adopted it was universally understood that a woman could not be appointed to a judicial office and this had been the accepted construction of the Constitution since;[1] likewise in 1890 they answered in the same tenor the question as to the eligibility of a woman as a notary.[2] A statute was subsequently passed allowing a woman to be a special commissioner, and giving such commissioners practically the power of justices of the peace. This was a clever move to dodge the issue. In 1913 the question of allowing women to be notaries was submitted to the people in the form of a constitutional amendment, but the people defeated it.

## The Power of Appointment and Removal

Originally, militia officers could only be removed by court martial or address[3] but Article IV of the Amendments provided that the Legislature should prescribe for the appointing of the commissary-general and for removing all commissioned officers. If the Legislature prescribes a definite term of office for an adjutant-general the Governor cannot remove him within that time.[4] Article IV of Chapter I, Section I, gave the Legislature the power to provide for the appointment of all civil officers not provided for in the Constitution. Thus, as various offices, heads of departments

[1] 107 *Mass.*, 604.

[2] 150 *Mass.*, 586.

[3] *Constitution of Massachusetts*, Chap. II, § I, Art. X.

[4] 216 *Mass.*, 605.

and boards and commissions have been established, the Governor has been given the power of appointment subject as a rule to confirmation by the Council, and the length of their tenure and method of removal has been established.

Originally, the secretary, treasurer and receiver-general, the commissary-general, notaries public and naval officers, were chosen annually by joint ballot of the senators and representatives.[1] The first change in the Constitution affecting these officers came in 1820 when Article IV of the Amendments provided that vacancies in the office of secretary and of treasurer occurring during the recess of the General Court should be filled by the Governor and Council and should hold good until the legislators met and appointed some one. In 1855 [2] another amendment was adopted by which these officers were to be elected by the people, along with the auditor, whose office had been established in 1849 [3] and the attorney-general who had originally been appointed by the Governor,[4] and in case of vacancy the General Court to fill the vacancy by joint ballot if in session, and if not in session then the Governor with consent of the Council to appoint.

## The Veto Power

The Governor must sign all warrants for the issuance of money from the treasury and all commissions of appointment with consent of the Council.[5] He has a veto over all bills passed by the Legislature but this can be over-ridden by a two-thirds vote of each House. Does this mean two-

[1] *Constitution of Massachusetts*, Chap. II, § IV, Art. I.

[2] Article of Amendment XVII. See the *Revised Laws*, Chaps. V and VI, for the duties of these officers.

[3] Chapter 56 of the *Acts* of 1849 provided for an Auditor to be chosen by joint ballot of the Legislature.

[4] *Constitution of Massachusetts*, Chap. II, § I, Art. IX.

[5] 211 *Mass.*, 632.

thirds of the actual membership of these bodies or merely two-thirds of those present and voting? The Constitution says clearly that it must be two-thirds of the members present in the second chamber. Rulings of presiding officers of the House and Senate have held that it means those present in both cases and authorities support this position. There is also, however, some authority the other way.[1]

The original draft of the Constitution provided for an absolute veto, but the Convention rejected this clause and substituted the two-thirds provision. The Governor is allowed five days after a bill or resolve has been laid before him in which to veto it. If he vetoes a measure and the General Court adjourns within five days, thereby preventing him from returning it with his objections to the House where it originated, the measure does not become a law.[2] There is no duty imposed on the Governor to return it when the Legislature reconvenes. The measure has become absolutely void.[3] A veto sent in while the Governor is out of the Commonwealth, but at his order and dictated by him before leaving, is valid.[4] A measure sent from the House or Senate to the Secretary of State cannot be held to have been laid before the Governor.[5] Presentation of a measure at the office of the Governor in presence of the person in charge is sufficient though the Governor is absent.[6] Many other interesting questions occur to us in connection with this veto provision. For instance, do the five days refer to days on which the Legislature sits or are all days included? If so, do holidays and Sundays count?

[1] See the rulings as printed in the *Manual for the General Court.*

[2] Article of Amendment I.

[3] 254 Vroom (*N. J.*), 303.

[4] *Opinions of the Judges*, 135 *Mass.*, 594.

[5] *Ibid.*, 99 *Mass.*, 636.

[6] *Ibid.*, 45 *N. H.*, 607.

There have been rulings by the Massachusetts Supreme Judicial Court in adjudicated cases and in *ex parte* opinions which throw some light on the subject. Probably legislative days alone count to make up the five days allowed for a veto and not calendar days,[1] and (in 112 *Mass.*, 59) Justice Morton said: "When a Statute fixes a limitation of time within which a particular act may or may not be done, if the time limited exceeds a week, Sunday is included in the computation; but if it is less than a week, Sunday is excluded. This is the established rule of interpretation in this State."

The power of veto is a high and important prerogative. It cannot be delegated. It must be performed strictly according to the provisions of the Constitution. Thus a veto message left on the fifth day upon the desk of the clerk of the branch of the Legislature in which the bill originated, but after the session is over for the day and the office of the clerk has been closed in the ordinary course of business and he and his assistants have gone, is not valid.[2]

This is a very interesting subject and one might weave suppositious cases around it for an indefinite time, but there are other important powers placed on the shoulders of the chief executive and we must pass on to them.

## The Right to Require Judicial Opinions

Among the unusual provisions in the Constitution of Massachusetts is the right given the Governor and Council to require opinions of the justices of the Supreme Judicial Court. They are given that authority and so is each branch of the Legislature.[3] This Article was suggested by the prac-

[1] *Opinions of the Judges*, 3 *Mass.*, 567.

[2] *Tuttle v.* Boston, 215 *Mass.*, 57, and cases cited.

[3] *Constitution of Massachusetts*, Chap. III, Art. II. A few other states have this provision, for example, Colorado, New Hampshire, Maine and

tice under the English Constitution allowing the King and Lords to demand the opinion of the twelve judges of England.[1] The authority being given to the Governor and Council, the Governor alone cannot require an opinion.[2] Nor, for the same reason, can the Council, acting alone, require one. These opinions, moreover, may be asked only on important questions of law and on solemn occasions.[3] The framers of the Constitution did not mean to have the judges called upon to answer indiscriminate questions. Thus the Court has held that this clause of the Constitution does not apply to questions of fact [4] and that it applies to questions of law only when such questions are actually before the body asking the opinion.[5] As the Court says: "The opinion of the Justices can be required only upon 'important questions of law' not upon questions of fact 'and upon solemn occasions': that is to say, when such questions of law are necessary to be determined by the body making the inquiry, in the exercise of the legislative or executive power entrusted to it by the Constitution and laws of the Commonwealth." [6]

In giving opinions the judges act not as a Court but as advisers. They are not bound by their opinion if the question comes up later in actual litigation. Consequently opinions are given by them with more freedom as individuals and there is less restraint against filing dissenting opinions.[7]

Rhode Island. Questions may be submitted by the Governor on matters affecting the State Constitution, in Florida, and on important questions of law, in South Dakota. (Stimson, *Federal and State Constitutions*, § 652.)

[1] *Opinions of the Judges*, 126 *Mass.*, 561.

[2] *Ibid.*, 214 *Mass.*, 602.

[3] *Ibid.*, 211 *Mass.*, 630.

[4] *Ibid.*, 120 *Mass.*, 600.

[5] *Ibid.*, 148 *Mass.*, 623; 150 *Mass.*, 598; and 217 *Mass.*, 607.

[6] *Ibid.*, 126 *Mass.*, 566.

[7] *Ibid.*, 214 *Mass.*, 599.

## The Power of Pardon

The Governor has the power of pardoning offenses by and with the advice of the Council. The Governor alone cannot pardon, nor can the Council. Favorable action by both is requisite and the initiative must come from the Governor as the Council can only get jurisdiction over a petition for pardon if sent to it by him.[1] The powers of the two are well expressed by the Court in an important decision.[1] "As to this class of cases, where the Constitution declares that the power to act is in the Governor, or that the act may be done by the Governor, 'by and with the advice of council,' or 'by and with the advice and consent of the council,' we are of opinion that the responsibility rests primarily upon the Governor to determine, as the supreme executive magistrate, whether any action is called for, and what action, if any, is desirable; and that the provision for advice of the Council is a requirement that their approval and concurrence shall accompany the affirmative act and enter into it before it becomes complete and effective. We do not think that these different phrases used in different parts of the Constitution, namely, 'by and with the advice of council,' 'by and with the advice and consent of the council,' 'with the advice and consent of the council,' 'with advice of council,' and 'with advice of the council,' differ at all in legal effect. They all recognize the fact that the act, first of all, and afterwards for all time, is to be the act of the Governor."

The power of pardon does not extend to persons convicted by impeachment. Nor will a pardon granted after commission of an offense but before conviction, be valid.[2]

[1] 190 *Mass.*, 616. [2] 109 *Mass.*, 323.

## The Power of Extradition

There are certain other privileges connected with the office of the chief executive which, though not covered in the State Constitution, are well recognized and important powers. Among these, the power of extradition is of great importance. This authority to return a fugitive from justice to the State that demands him is governed by a clause in the United States Constitution,[1] by federal Statute and by comity between the different States. The Revised Statutes of the United States, (Section 5278), provide: "Whenever the Executive authority of any State or Territory demands any person as a fugitive from justice, of the executive authority of any State or Territory to which such person has fled, and produces a copy of an *indictment* found or an *affidavit* made before a magistrate of any State or Territory, charging the person demanded with having committed treason, felony, or other crime, certified as authentic by the Governor or chief magistrate of the State or Territory from whence the person so charged has fled it shall be the duty of said executive to cause the person demanded to be arrested etc."

There is, however, no way of enforcing extradition if the Governor of the State refuses to grant it.

An indictment is necessary or a complaint setting forth the facts and accompanied by an affidavit. Generally speaking, it is necessary to show that the offense charged is a crime in the demanding State, that the accused was there at the time the crime was committed, and that he is now in Massachusetts.[2] In other words, that the person demanded has been substantially charged with a crime and is a fugitive from justice.[3]

[1] *Constitution of the United States*, Art. IV, § 2.

[2] *Report of the Attorney-General*, 1912, p. 220.

[3] 196 *United States*, 372.

Though a State can lay down additional provisions and regulations applying to a petition for the rendition of a prisoner from another State, it cannot hold any other State subject to those conditions provided the general rules above stated have been complied with. An Attorney-General of Massachusetts has held that "extradition papers from a foreign State which comply with the laws of the United States and also with the Statutes of the demanding State, are sufficient to authorize the Governor to surrender the fugitive demanded although said papers do not comply with the Massachusetts statute requiring affidavits by persons having actual knowledge of the offence charged." [1]

As a result of an interstate extradition conference held in New York in 1887, the States adopted certain rules of procedure to govern in extradition cases. Under these rules the rights of any person who is held for extradition may be safeguarded by suing out a writ of habeas corpus. This proceeding was followed in the recent Thaw case in New Hampshire.

### The Governor Not Subject to Mandamus

So far we have been discussing the powers of the chief executive to perform certain acts. Let us for a moment consider the matter from the other point of view. Suppose he refuses to perform his duties or some particular one. Is there any way of compelling him to take action? In some States of the Union, the courts hold that a writ of mandamus may be issued to compel a Governor or other public officer to perform a particular act, provided it is purely ministerial, requiring no discretion, whereas it is well established that such a writ will not issue where the exercise of discretion or judgment is required. In Massachusetts it has been decided

[1] *Opinions of the Attorney General*, vol. 1, 1891–98, p. 116.

that a writ of mandamus will not be issued against the Governor to compel him to perform any of his official duties. This is according to the weight of authority. The court says: "It seems better to hold that, for whatever he does officially, the Governor shall answer only to his own conscience, to the people who elected him, and in case of the possible commission of a high crime or misdemeanor, to a court of impeachment."[1]

## Incompatibility of Offices

No Governor or Lieutenant-Governor may hold any other office under the Commonwealth or receive any pension or salary from any other State or government.[2] This makes it illegal for the Governor or Lieutenant-Governor to hold even the office of justice of the peace or notary public, or to act as counsel on a salary for any other government or to hold any other inconsistent offices of this nature.[3]

## State Laws and Treaty Obligations

There is one other subject to which I want to refer briefly before closing this chapter. It is of peculiar importance at the present time when the recent discussion about California's excluding the Japanese from rights enjoyed by other aliens, is ringing in our ears. This is the question of State laws being subordinate to treaty rights. It is of course one belonging to the field of constitutional law and any complete discussion of it must be left to books on that general subject. There one can find a presentation of possible limitations on treaty-making powers, of whether matters can be legally included in treaties which would be unconstitutional if

[1] 207 *Mass.*, 577.
[2] *Constitution of Massachusetts*, Chap. VI, Art. II.
[3] 123 *Mass.*, 525.

dealt with by Congress, of how far States can go in passing infringing legislation, and other matters germane to this subject. Suffice it to say here that it is unquestioned that when the law of a State covering subject matters not reserved to the States conflicts with a treaty made by the United States, the latter is supreme.

The same is probably true of a State law covering a matter ordinarily reserved for State legislation. As Professor Willoughby says: "The author is convinced that the ***obiter*** doctrine that the reserved rights of the States may never be infringed upon by the treaty-making power will sooner or later be frankly repudiated by the Supreme Court. In its place will be definitely stated the doctrine that in all that properly relates to international rights and obligations, whether these rights and obligations rest upon the general principles of international law or have been conventionally created by specific treaties, the United States possesses all the powers of a constitutionally centralized sovereign State; and, therefore, when the necessity from the international standpoint arises the treaty-making power may be exercised, even though thereby the rights ordinarily reserved to the States are invaded." [1]

A recent decision in Massachusetts states distinctly that where the provisions of a treaty conflict with the State law or the Constitution of the State, the treaty is supreme.[2]

[1] *Constitutional Laws of the United States* (Students' Ed.), p. 173.
[2] 191 *Mass.*, 278.

# CHAPTER VII

## LEGISLATIVE PROCEDURE

To become law a measure has to pass through three readings in each branch of the Legislature; it must be engrossed and enacted in each, and then must be signed by the Governor, or left for five days without his signature, or vetoed within the required period and passed over his veto.

### Filing Petitions and Bills

When one looks at the Massachusetts "blue books" which are issued yearly with their mass of laws general and special, one seldom pauses to reflect on the hearings, debates, readings and contests which must have taken place, and upon the general machinery that had to be set in motion before these matters were in shape to be put in the statute book. The fact that the Legislature sits for many months each year and steadily grinds out laws, is of course common knowledge. But if the average citizen wanted to get an idea enacted into law, would he know how to go about it? He would probably consult a lawyer. This lawyer would undoubtedly know the method of procedure by which to set the ball rolling, but unless he had been at some time in the State government or had special experience with legislation he would scarcely know how to draw a bill and its accompanying petition in scientific form. For instance, very few realize the value of making the petition as broad as possible. Since each petition must, under the rules, be accompanied by a bill, the phrase commonly used in a petition is to ask "for legislation according to the accompanying bill." Generally speaking, nothing could be more unwise than this. Events will undoubtedly occur making it desirable to amend the bill. If it is desired to cut out some of its provisions or to limit its scope well and good; the petition will be broad enough for that. But if, as is more often the case, it is sought to enlarge the bill's scope and to increase its requirements, then one bumps right up against the limited wording of the petition. It is true, of course, that many bills are reported by committees and go through both branches despite the fact that they contain provisions which are beyond the scope of the petitions originally accompanying them. But this is either because of inadvertence or because the bill is so unimportant that no opposition to it develops.

A point of order, moreover, cannot be upheld on this score after a measure has reached a certain stage. This is true, for instance, if the bill has gone to a third reading [1] or been substituted for the adverse report of a committee [2] or passed through the other branch of the Legislature.[3] These rulings are based on the theory that the discrepancy has been ratified by the action of the legislators and though in the last case the ratification is by the members of the other house, courtesy between the two branches governs.

## Petitions Should be Broad in Scope

A bill broader than the scope of a petition may be saved from an adverse ruling (1) by another petition which happens to be before the committee, or (2) by some clause in a message of the Governor or in the report of some State officer or department or board, on which it can be based. It

[1] "Notes of Rulings on the House Rules," Rule 30, ¶ 2. These "Notes of Rulings" are printed in the *Manual for the General Court.*

[2] *Ibid.*, Rule 47, ¶ 3.

[3] "Notes of Rulings on the Senate Rules," Rule 23, and citations.

is not well to trust to luck in these matters, however. All difficulties can be best obviated by framing the petition broadly. Thus if one wants to have a law passed increasing the number of judges petition "for legislation relating to the judiciary" and your bill can then be framed or amended at will to cover the number of judges, their powers, duties or anything else. It need not even be limited to any particular court. Any legislation relating to judges would be germane to such a petition.

In the same way, if one wants a law passed increasing the stock of a street railway company or extending its franchise rights in any other manner, there is no need of stating any specific request in the petition. The bill will state specifically what you want; and if the petition merely asks for legislation relative to street railways, then the bill can be amended or expanded at will.

## How Bills are Introduced

There are several ways of getting proposed legislation before the two Houses. The most common is by filing with the clerk of the Senate or with the clerk of the House a petition accompanied by a bill. Another way is to have a bill introduced on leave. This means that the petitioner is a member of the General Court and he asks leave to introduce the bill. It is a purely formal matter, the presiding officer merely stating the fact that the Senator from such and such a county, or that Representative so and so, asks leave to introduce the following bill, and then the clerk reads the title of the bill, the vote on granting leave being taken as a perfunctory matter during routine business at the opening of the day's session.

In the case of a petition accompanied by a bill the petition must be signed by some citizen of the Commonwealth, and not necessarily by a legislator; but before being read in either legislative hall it must be endorsed on the outside as being presented by some member of the House or Senate. This does not mean that the member of the House or Senate advocates the passage of the bill, as it does in the case of a measure introduced on leave; it is merely an endorsement required by the rules of procedure in Massachusetts. I remember during one of the years when I was Speaker of the House of Representatives a petition was handed to the clerk for the impeachment of a certain judge. The clerk brought it in his tin box to the desk and said he could not get any Representative to permit the endorsement of his name to it; so the paper lay there day after day and as no member of the House was ever secured to attach his name to it, the measure was never introduced.

A third way of getting a bill before the Legislature is for a member to rise and move that a certain matter be taken from the files. This means that every year certain matters are "referred to the next General Court," and when in the following year a member rises and asks to have a measure taken from the files he refers to one of these. The motion is put and carried as a matter of course, as nobody ever raises an objection.

Any of these three methods, when used, must be initiated before five o'clock in the afternoon of the second Saturday of the session. Petitions or bills coming in after that time go under the rules to the next General Court.[1] This rule can be suspended only by a four-fifths vote of members of each branch present and voting, and where the petition is not accompanied by a bill or resolve embodying the legislation requested it requires unanimous consent to suspend the

[1] Joint Rules of the Senate and House of Representatives, Rule 12. These are also printed in the *Manual for the General Court.*

rule. The rule does not apply to petitions in support of legislation or remonstrances against legislation already pending, nor in certain other cases of an unusual nature. Nor does it apply to what I shall call a fourth method of getting laws passed. This is to base legislative proposals on some recommendation in a message of the Governor, or some report of one of the State officers, or of one of the boards or commissions or departments of the State, or of a committee or commission that has been appointed to sit and report to the General Court. Recommendations contained in a message or in the reports of these departments, boards or commissions, form a basis on which a bill or resolve can be put before the Legislature by the committee to which these documents are referred. These reports are supposed to be on hand when the Legislature meets, but they very seldom get in until some time later, and of course the Governor can send in a message at any time during the session.

## The Committee on Rules

Requests for legislation under the first three methods coming in after five o'clock of the second Saturday are referred under the rule to the Committee on Rules. This committee sits and hears the reasons why the proposals for legislation were not filed in time. If the excuse seems sufficient or the matter is of great importance the committee may vote to recommend suspension of the rules, and the House or Senate, whichever branch it may be that has the question under consideration, usually follows such report.

Motions to suspend the ninth Joint Rule must also go to the Committee on Rules. The ninth Joint Rule provides that petitions asking for certain legislation like the incorporation of a town or city, of a railroad or street railway, canal or company for building structures over navigable waters, or the incorporation of an educational institution, shall, unless notice required by Chapter III of the Revised Laws or other laws has been given, be referred to the next General Court.

The Rules Committee of the House does not have the broad discretion to recommend suspension of this rule that it does in the case of the twelfth Joint Rule. It must report adversely on the suspension of the ninth Joint Rule[1] unless the members are satisfied by the evidence produced that the petitioners have given notice by public advertisement or otherwise, equivalent to that required by Chapter III of the Revised Laws.[2] The Senate Rules contain no such provision as this.

The Committee on Rules is a powerful body. The presiding officer of each branch sits in that branch as chairman of the Committee and the leading members of the Senate and House make up its membership. Many other matters besides motions to suspend the ninth and twelfth Joint Rules go to it under the rules. Thus all orders authorizing committees to travel or to employ stenographers, or involving special investigations, or providing that information be transmitted, must be referred without debate to the Committee on Rules, and the Committee on Rules must report upon such matters within fourteen days.[2]

The joint Rules also provide that where legislation affects the rights of individuals, or of private or municipal corporations otherwise than as it affects generally the people of the Commonwealth or the people of the city or town to which it applies, a petition is always necessary to introduce such matter, and that no bill or resolve shall be reported on such

[1] Also House Rule 32 and Senate Rule 25 which contain provisions similar to Joint Rule 9.

[2] House Rule 104.

petition until the Committee is satisfied that proper notice has been given to all parties by public advertisement or otherwise, or that all parties interested have waived notice in writing. Objection to the violation of this rule may be made at any stage prior to the third reading.[1]

### The Reference of Bills to Committees

All bills and resolves, except "money bills" about which there is a special provision that they must originate in the House of Representatives,[2] annual and special reports and other requests for legislation, may start in either the House or the Senate; but reports or legislation based on them have to go sooner or later to both branches. They are first entered on a docket by the clerks of the branch receiving them, and arranged neatly; then they are brought in by the clerks in a tin box to the Senate or House as the case may be, and handed to the President of the Senate or to the Speaker, who, after reading out the titles of the various bills, refer them to whatever committee is deemed the appropriate one to consider each of them. Generally speaking, there is no objection to the off-hand assignment of these bills as made by the President or by the Speaker. Matters relating to street railways go naturally to the street railway committee, and those relating to taxation to the committee on taxation, and it is usually too clear for argument which committee should have jurisdiction.

But now and then matters arise which might appropriately be sent to either of two committees, and if they are of importance, and if the sponsors of the bill particularly desire reference to a certain committee, there may be a discussion and contest as to what committee should have it. In such event the assignment made by the presiding officer

[1] Joint Rule 8. [2] Joint Rule 4.

is contested from the floor and may possibly be overruled by a majority of the members present. After the matters have been referred to committees they are duly placed upon the committee dockets and advertised for hearings.

## How Legislative Committees are Selected

In Massachusetts committees are appointed by the presiding officers,— in the Senate by the President of the Senate, and in the House by the Speaker of the House. The Senator or Representative first named on each committee acts as chairman. In the case of Joint Committees the Senator first named is the chairman. Clerks are elected by the committees from their own members, and these clerks, after consulting with the chairman, attend to arranging dates for the hearings and advertising in the newspapers matters to be heard. Committees are announced by the presiding officers just as soon as the bodies are organized by the election of officers. When I first went to the Legislature, however, in 1901, committees were often not announced for a week or ten days, but it soon became customary to announce committees the first day.

Each branch has besides a presiding officer and clerk, a chaplain. He like the others is nominated in party caucus and elected by the members. As a rule the nominees of the Republican caucus are elected, Republicans being in the majority. The sergeant-at-arms is elected by concurrent vote, he being an officer of both branches. The clerk of each branch appoints his assistants and so does the sergeant-at-arms. In the roster of assistants to the sergeant-at-arms are included watchmen, elevator men, pages, door-keepers, and so on. Hence he has a great deal of patronage and as the civil service rules do not apply to these appointments the sergeant-at-arms is a powerful man.

The Speaker of the House appoints also eight monitors, two for each of the four divisions of the House, one Democrat and one Republican in each division. These men, when a standing vote is taken, count the members that rise in favor and those that rise against the proposition, and announce the result, which is tabulated by the clerk and handed to the Speaker. In the Senate no monitors are appointed, because the membership is so small it is quite possible for the clerk to make the count.

## Standing and Joint Standing Committees

There are standing committees of the Senate and standing committees of the House as well as joint standing committees of the two bodies. The standing committees of the Senate are those on Judiciary, on Ways and Means, on Bills in the Third Reading, on Engrossed Bills, and on Rules. The standing committees of the House include committees covering these subjects and also a committee on Elections and one on Payroll. The Senate Committees are smaller than the House Committees, though in each branch the committees on Bills in the Third Reading and on Engrossed Bills consist of only three members. In the House the chairmen of the committees on Bills in the Third Reading and on Engrossed Bills have seats of honor at a desk at the left of the Speaker, the clerk and his assistant being at the right. Certain members, too, like the chairman of the Judiciary Committee, the chairman of the Ways and Means Committee, and the ranking member of the Rules Committee, have special seats assigned to them. So do the monitors. The senior member of the House and the oldest member who is not the senior member are allowed to select their seats. All the other members draw for seats,[1] the clerk

[1] In the Senate the President appoints a committee to assign seats.

calling the roll, and a committee of three made up from those who do not have to draw taking numbers out of a box as the names are called; the number drawn is the number of the member's seat unless an exchange is made and notice given to the sergeant-at-arms within five days from the day of the drawing. The drawing of seats takes place immediately after the appointment of committees and monitors.

### Work of the Joint Committees

The greater number of committees, of course, are joint committees; that is, committees made up of members of the House and Senate who sit jointly. There are twenty-nine of these committees in all and they start with a committee on Agriculture made up of three senators, the senator first named being the chairman of the whole committee, and eight representatives. The chairman on the part of the House is the representative first named among the House members. These committees include committees on the various appropriate subjects, sometimes consisting of eight men and sometimes in the case of busy and important committees — like the committees on Cities, on Insurance, on Legal Affairs, on Mercantile Affairs, on Metropolitan Affairs, on Public Institutions, on Public Lighting, on Railroads, on Street Railways,— of fifteen, and in the case of the two busiest, the joint committee on Ways and Means and on Judiciary, of sixteen.

Most of the business, naturally, is done by these joint standing committees and not by the standing committees of the separate branches. The committees on Rules and on Ways and Means seldom sit jointly. The committee on the Judiciary almost always sits jointly.[1] The House committees on Payroll and on Elections do not sit jointly

[1] See Joint Rule 1.

with any committees of the Senate as each branch has jurisdiction only over its own membership in such matters. The same is true of the committees on Engrossed Bills and on Bills in the Third Reading, as they have jurisdiction only over bills which have gone to engrossment or to a third reading in the branch in which they sit.

We have already noted that the Senate has no standing committees on Elections or on Payroll and that the House does have such committees. In the Senate it has been customary for the chairman of the Ways and Means Committee to present an order for the payroll, to be made up by the clerk. This procedure makes a committee on Payroll unnecessary. The pay of members, both for travelling and salary, is governed by statute; the provision as to travel is that each member receives two dollars a mile. Only one journey to and from the State House is computed. Boston, however, is regarded as being five miles from the State House and every Boston member gets $10, while representatives from North Adams at the farther end of the State receive mileage amounting to a substantial sum. The salary of each member of the House and Senate is fixed at $1,000, the presiding officer in each branch receiving $2,000. In case of a disputed election in the Senate, as there is no standing committee on Elections, a special committee is appointed to deal with the matter.

## Consideration of Measures by Committees

We have now seen how a bill is introduced and how it gets to a committee, as well as how the committees are made up. But before proceeding any further into a discussion of the rules, we must, to follow the passage of a measure properly, find what becomes of it after it has been referred to a committee.

If a committee to which a bill has been referred thinks it ought not to have the measure because some other committee can deal with it better or more appropriately or because such other committee has measures of a similar nature before it, the first committee may by vote ask to be discharged and the matter may be referred to another committee.

Let us assume the usual proceeding, however, where the bill, resolve, message or report is advertised for hearing on a certain date. After the hearing a committee often waits a long time, especially if the measure is an important one, before a vote is taken as to whether or not it should report favorably. If the vote is in favor of reporting a bill or resolve, a certain member of the committee is given charge of the measure. Those members of the committee who so desire may be recorded as dissenters from the report, and of course may fight the passage of the bill when it gets into the branch to which they belong. If the committee votes to report adversely upon a matter a member of the committee is given charge of this adverse report and those who so desire may be recorded as dissenters. They or any other member of the Senate or House may, when the report comes in, move to reject the adverse report and substitute the bill itself for this adverse report. In all cases, however, the measure must come out of the committee and go to either the Senate or the House.

But let us suppose that no vote is taken by the committee, either because it is difficult to get the members together, or because the measure is unimportant, or because the committee does not wish to take action. What happens under such circumstances?

Under the rules prevailing in our national government at Washington, and under the usual rules of procedure of the

State governments, the measure would stay in committee and thus be quietly killed; in those jurisdictions, unless a committee reports favorably on a measure, it never gets to the House or the Senate except of course when both of those bodies vote to instruct the committee to report the measure, and that is a very unusual proceeding. But in Massachusetts everything has to be reported from a committee whether the committee favors it or not; and we thus see one of the chief reasons why the sessions in Massachusetts are so much longer than in most other States. Where matters can be shelved in committee and thus prevented from reaching the legislative body, the bills which the latter has to act on will be naturally fewer and the time taken up in putting them through or in defeating them as well as that spent in lengthy discussions will be cut off.

In Massachusetts a rule of the Legislature[1] requires committees to report on all matters previously referred to them on or before the second Wednesday in March. This time may be extended until the second Wednesday in April. When that date has expired all measures still in the hands of any committees must be reported within three days by the chairman of the committee representing that branch of the Legislature in which the bills were introduced. The report must recommend that the bills be "referred to the next General Court"; and this rule can be suspended only by a four-fifths vote.[2]

Discussion may then take place on the measure and substitution of any bill for the report of the committee may prevail. As such reports are only perfunctory, being required by rule, and are not necessarily indications of the atti-

[1] Joint Rule 10.

[2] No recommittal of any matter to a committee can take place after the fourth Wednesday in March. Joint Rule 5.

tude of the committee, the substitution of bills may often prevail without opposition from the committee. We notice that this rule applies to matters referred to a committee before the second Wednesday in March. If, after that date, a message from the Governor is referred to a committee, or a measure is recommitted, or a report comes to them from a commission, the committee have an unlimited time to report thereon.

We notice too that this rule requires a report to that branch of the legislature in which the bill originated. In the case of reports made before the expiration of the time-limit there is a rule providing that joint committees may report to either branch in their discretion, having reference to an equal distribution of business between the two branches.[1] There are exceptions to this as to all other rules, and one of them is that "money bills" as we have previously seen, must be reported to the House.[2]

## Recess Committees

While discussing the subject of committees, I ought to say a word about Recess Committees and Committees of Conference.

Recess Committees are committees appointed by the presiding officers of the two Houses to sit during the recess of the Legislature for the purpose of investigating some particular subject and of reporting thereon. In some years a number of these committees are voted, and as the members are paid the burden of expense imposed on the Commonwealth may be a heavy one. Of course these committees may, by taking a load of details off the shoulders of the Legislature, save a great deal of time and accomplish beneficial results; but generally speaking, Recess Committees

[1] See Joint Rule 4. [2] See *above*, p. 96.

should be tabooed as they involve an expense without adequate compensation in service to the State. The abuse of the Recess Committee system usually takes care of itself, however, as popular protests are raised against the custom when it is frequently resorted to. Only one Recess Committee was appointed while I was Speaker. I strenuously opposed all others and had grave doubts about the advisability of that one. As the question it was to deal with was being bitterly fought in the Legislature and related to an important railway matter, namely a charter for a fast line between Boston and Providence which was being sought by three responsible and important business houses, the appointment of a Recess Committee seemed on the whole wise. The able report of this Recess Committee later justified the appointment.

Instead of having a Recess Committee, which is made up of members of the Legislature, it is often customary to refer matters of this sort (which have given committees and the Legislature much trouble during the session), to one of the State Boards or possibly to a special commission appointed for the purpose by the Governor and composed of experts who serve without pay. Reference to a State Board is the most usual plan as members of such boards or commissions are experts on their respective subjects and are already receiving salaries from the Commonwealth.

## Committees of Conference

Committees of Conference are committees appointed by the presiding officers to clear up disagreements between the two branches of the Legislature. For example, if a matter has gone through one branch and an amendment has been put on in the other branch in which the first branch fails to concur, some member who is interested in the legislation and thinks that possibly by talking the matter over in committee a compromise may be reached, can rise and move for a Committee of Conference between the two branches. If this vote prevails, then the President of the Senate and the Speaker of the House each appoint three members. A Conference report, if agreed to by a majority of each committee, must be made to the branch which asked for the conference.[1]

## The Committee of the Whole

There is still another kind of committee which should be noted. In Washington when the tariff or some such complicated matter is under discussion, the House of Representatives will resolve itself into a Committee of the Whole. The object of this is to give the members a greater freedom by making debate informal. The proceedings do not go on a journal, and a chairman is elected to take the place of the regular presiding officer. To make the sitting still mcre informal the chairman sits at the clerk's desk. In dealing with complicated questions much benefit is gained by going into Committee of the Whole. In State governments there is little need for such procedure, and in Massachusetts it is seldom if ever resorted to.

## Joint Conventions

Just as we have Joint Committees and Committees of Conference between the two branches of the Legislature, so we have Joint Conventions in which the two branches sit together as one body in the House of Representatives and are presided over by the President of the Senate. Such joint meetings take place when the Governor of Massachusetts is inaugurated and so occur once a year, at least.

[1] Joint Rule 11.

They are also held by special vote whenever some distinguished person comes to address the Legislature, or to be received by the Legislature, and they used to be held for the election of United States senators when such Senators were chosen by joint ballot of the House and Senate.

## How Bills are Reported

But let us now return to our bill and petition for legislation which was left before a committee. If a hearing has been held and both sides have been given an opportunity to be heard (in case any one desires to be heard), the committee may, after the hearings for the day have been closed, go into what is called "executive session" and vote on this and other matters. As a rule, however, executive sessions are held at certain stated intervals, say every Thursday, and matters that have been heard are then taken up for decision. This gives due notice to committee members that any bills on which hearings have been closed may be discussed and voted on at that time.

If our bill or resolve is voted on favorably, it is then given to one of the members of the committee to report to the House or to the Senate. This member takes it to the clerk of that branch of which he is a member, the clerk makes a record of it and hands it to the presiding officer among other reports of committees.

## Proceedings in the Legislature

The order of proceedings in the legislative session is first for the presiding officer to take the chair, when he says, "The hour to which the House stands adjourned having arrived, the House will now be in order"; then he remarks, "Prayer will now be offered by the chaplain." Then he asks for "petitions, memorials, remonstrances and papers of a like nature."[1] Reports of committees are then taken up, together with matters coming from the other branch. The latter may be measures that have taken their several readings there or they may be adverse reports that have been accepted and sent over for concurrence. They may also be notices of rejection of legislation which had already gone through one branch.

All these proceedings take place before the calendar containing what are called "the orders of the day" is taken up. This calendar of course does not exist at the opening of the session but gradually comes into being as reports come from committees. Before the calendar is taken up, too, motions for reconsideration must be made. The rules provide that "no motion to reconsider a vote shall be entertained unless it is made on the same day on which the vote was passed or before the orders of the day have been taken up on the next day thereafter on which a quorum is present."[2]

In presenting the reports of committees to the House the clerk reads off the list in this manner: — report of the committee on so and so, "leave to withdraw," or, "ought not to pass," or "no legislation necessary" or "reference to next General Court,"[3] or else that the committee on so and so "report the accompanying bill" or "report the accompanying resolve" as the case may be. In the first contingency, that is, in case the report was adverse, the presiding officer

[1] These may come in at any time during the session if they relate to pending legislation. See Joint Rule 12.

[2] See House Rule 70.

[3] These expressions are technical. When a committee reports adversely on a bill accompanied by a petition the term used is "leave to withdraw"; when against a bill which has been introduced on leave "ought not to pass"; when against a message of the Governor, or of a State Department or a Board or Commission "no legislation necessary" while the expression "next General Court" is applicable to anything.

merely says, "Placed in the orders of the day for tomorrow." In the second contingency, where a bill or resolve is reported, he says, "First reading of the bill," if it is a bill, or of a "resolve," if it is a resolve, and then says, "placed in the orders of the day for tomorrow." This first reading takes place as a matter of course and without debate.

## Special Procedure in the Case of Bills for Raising or for Appropriating Money

Right here it might be well to state that rules governing the reference of measures involving state and county money are somewhat different in the Senate and House. In the Senate *all* such matters, both State and County, are referred to its Committee on Ways and Means, except those reported from the joint committee of that name. In the House jurisdiction is divided. Measures concerning state money are sent to the Committee on Ways and Means, and those providing for the expenditure of county money are referred to the Committee on Counties, which under House Rule 44 is termed the "Committee on Counties on the part of the House." Of course any measure reported to the House from the Joint Committee on Counties would not be so referred, as the House members have already passed upon it in joint committee. If then, a measure is reported dealing with appropriations, that is contemplating an expenditure of public money or grant of public property, the presiding officer refers it to the Committee on Ways and Means. In the House if it involves an expenditure of county money he refers it after its first reading to the Committee on Counties on the part of the House. Neither of these committees is supposed to add any new provisions unless they are directly connected with the financial features.[1]

[1] House Rule 44.

When a measure is reported by the Committee on Ways and Means or by the Committee on Counties on the part of the House as well as by another committee, the names of two members appear in the calendar as in charge of the measure, that is the name of the member who was given charge of it for the original committee which made the report. and the member in charge from the Finance Committee. So also when it goes to the other branch it is in charge of the chairmen of the two committees if a hearing was held before the *Joint* Committee on Ways and Means; and if not it will be in charge of the chairman of the committee originally reporting the bill for that committee and whoever is given the assignment from the Finance Committee. But suppose the report of the Finance Committee is adverse? Then the members in charge for each committee appear against each other, leading the contestants pro or con.

## Stages in Passing Bills

But to return to our bill before the House. When the calendar is reached the next day it is read over, item by item, by the presiding officer and if any member wishes to discuss any matter on the calendar, he calls out "pass." Matters which are not "passed," in this way are disposed of then and there by being given a reading or by being rejected. The calendar being read through, the presiding officer turns back to the first matter which he has marked in pencil with a "P" for "passed." As a rule discussion takes place, though of course a member may merely have called out "pass" in order to give himself the opportunity of investigating the measure and may find that he does not wish to oppose it.

Now when our matter is reached the question comes either on accepting the report of the committee in case its report was adverse, or else of passing the bill to a third reading. Suppose the first contingency has taken place, namely, an adverse report: If the members vote to accept the report of the committee the matter is held twenty-four hours for possible reconsideration and then sent to the other branch. A member may, however, rise and move to substitute the bill for the adverse report of the committee and the question is then put in some such form as this: "The Senator from Suffolk, or Mr. So and So of Boston, moves to substitute for the report of the Committee on Agriculture, leave to withdraw, the following bill." The bill is then read by the clerk, but only by its title, of course.

If the motion to substitute is rejected the question then comes on accepting the adverse report of the committee and after failure of the first motion acceptance is of course assured.[1] If substitution prevails, however, then the bill is given a first reading just as if it had originally come in from the committee.[2] It then takes its place in the orders of the day for the next day (unless, of course, it is a financial measure and has to go to the Committee on Ways and Means or the Committee on Counties.)[3] It is now on the calendar for its second reading and this is the first stage at which discussion of a bill on its merits is allowed. When the bill is reached on the calendar the presiding officer says, "Second reading of the bill." The clerk reads the bill by its title and the presiding officer then says, "This bill has been read a second time. Question on ordering it to a third reading." If there is to be any discussion the members now rise one after the other and put forth their views. They are recognized in the order in which they stand up and catch the eye

[1] Rejection after this motion to substitute is a "final rejection." As to the difference between these two cases, see *below*, pp. 126–128.

[2] House Rule 43.

[3] See *above*, p. 108.

of the chair, except that those who have not spoken on the question are given a preference over those who have, and those on the opposite side of the question from the preceding speaker are preferred to those who desire to speak on the same side. Often when a big debate is expected, the presiding officer is furnished by the leaders on each side of the question with the names of those whom they expect to speak. This simplifies the task of recognizing members pro and con alternately, and of dividing the time equally between the two sides.

## Votes and Roll Calls

If any one desires to raise a point of order that the bill is broader than the scope of the petition this is the stage at which to do so. But suppose the debate is over and no point of order has been raised or if raised has been overruled. The chair then puts the question. If the voice vote is overwhelming, or if there has been little or no contest the matter may end there. If not, a rising vote is demanded. All those in favor are then asked to rise and the monitors return the count. Then those opposed are asked to rise and the count is declared. If the vote is still close or if there is a desire to carry the matter further and get the members on record, a roll-call is demanded. The presiding officer now says, "All those in favor of ordering the yeas and nays will please stand." To obtain a roll-call in the House thirty members must rise; in the Senate one-fifth of the members present. The monitors now return the count unless so many members rise that all doubt is removed, in which case the chair merely takes matters into his own hands and announces that "more than thirty members having joined in the call the yeas and nays are ordered." Of course if less than the required number rise, no roll-call is ordered and the standing vote prevails. But if the requisite number demand a roll-call the clerk gets out his list containing the names of the members. Before the roll is called the "pairs" should be announced. This is done by a member rising in his place and saying, "I am paired with Mr.——, of ——, if he were here he would vote yes; I vote no" or vice versa. On matters requiring more than a majority vote, such as a constitutional amendment in the House, or the passing of a measure over the Governor's veto or the suspension of the rules pairs are allowed; but they should not be as the votes in such cases are not equal and ought not to be so reckoned. Unless a rule is made against pairing it is a difficult practice to discourage as members do not like to refuse when asked by other members to pair. The chair now asks, "Have all pairs been announced?" If he receives no response he says "the clerk will now call the roll." The names are called off alphabetically, and each member present should answer yes or no when his name is called. I have known members to leave their seats, however, or remain in the lobby so as to avoid voting, and on one occasion a member sitting near me had a page bring him a fake message calling him away from the chamber. The member had promised to vote for the resolve but had changed his mind and sent himself a telegram so as to have an excuse for going outside and side-stepping the vote. Weak men often change their minds when they see that they are on the losing side. When the roll has been called those who wish to change their votes may rise and ask how they are recorded, and if they claim to have been recorded erroneously they may ask to be recorded the other way. The clerk now counts the votes pro and con, and hands the result to the presiding officer. The latter announces the result by saying: "On this question so many members having voted in the affirmative and so many in the negative the bill is ordered to a third reading." Or if the negatives prevail he varies this last clause by saying: "and the bill is rejected." If the vote is a tie, or the chair's vote would make it a tie, or if for any other reason the chair desires to vote he asks the clerk to call his name before the vote is announced. There is no rule requiring the presiding officer to be recorded, however.

## The Committee on Bills in the Third Reading

The bill or resolve now having been ordered to a third reading, it is so endorsed by the clerk and by him sent to the Committee on Bills in the Third Reading.[1] It goes to this committee for examination, correction and report. The bill or resolve appears as a matter of course in the calendar for the next day; but when it is reached on the calendar, if it has not been returned to the clerk the presiding officer passes it by, remarking merely that the matter is still in the hands of the Committee on Bills in the Third Reading.

There is no rule limiting the time this committee can hold a measure, but a reasonable time is assumed. Of course the presiding officer will urge on this committee as on all others, to hurry up and report matters; but persuasion is not always sufficiently effective. On one occasion when the so-called "Boston Caucus Act" was before the Legislature there was an attempt to stall the legislation in this way. The measure had gone through the House after a long drawn out contest, the Boston Democrats being solidly against it. On reaching the hands of the Committee on Bills in the Third Reading in the Senate, which was made up of two Democrats and one Republican, the bill mysteriously disappeared, and nobody could find it. It was too late to introduce a new measure under the rules, and with so much

[1] Senate Rule 33; House Rule 50.

opposition there was no possibility of getting a four-fifths vote to suspend the rules. There happened to be other petitions, however, which had been before the Committee on Election Laws, relating to this same subject. Another bill similar to the one that had disappeared was quickly drawn up and presented to the House, based on one of these petitions; and this time when it reached the Senate due care was taken to see that it did not vanish from sight.

When the Committee on Bills in the Third Reading have finished their scrutiny of the bill they return it to that branch of which they are members, and the bill then comes up for another reading. The chief work of the committee lies in correcting the spelling and grammatical mistakes in the bill and sometimes re-drafting it to make the English correct. If they do more than this and should change the sense of the bill, or make any material change these alterations must be reported in the shape of amendments, to be separately printed and to appear in the calendar.[1]

The measure being again in the jurisdiction of the House, the presiding officer when it is reached in the calendar says "Third reading of the bill." The clerk then reads the bill by its title only, and the Speaker puts the question thus: "This bill has been read three times and is reported by the Committee on Bills in the Third Reading to be correctly drawn; question on passing it to be engrossed; those in favor say 'aye' those opposed 'no'; the 'ayes' have it." Debate, if any, at this stage and the voting, in case of a count or a roll-call, take place as previously explained.[2] The measure is now held twenty-four hours in order to allow time for reconsideration. Then it is sent to the other

[1] Senate Rule 33; House Rule 26. See also Rulings on House Rules under Rule 50. It is within the province of the Committee on Bills in the Third Reading, to report that a bill ought not to pass.

[2] See *above*, pp. 110–113.

branch and if it came originally from a joint committee as most bills do, it at once takes a reading and goes into the orders of the day for the following day. Of course if it came from a committee of one branch alone it must be referred to the like committee of the other branch, or if it is a bill involving the expenditure of money and has not been acted on by the Committee on Ways and Means of both branches, it must be referred to that committee for action and report. Generally speaking, however, the bill goes into the orders of the day for the next day, and then takes its several readings in the same way as in the first branch, as already described.

### Suspending the Rules to Expedite Bills

Under the rules, bills are read only by their titles unless a special request to have them read in full is made by some member, or unless they are put through under suspension of the rules. Under suspension of the rules a bill may be put through all its stages in five minutes. This is done by a member's rising and asking to have all rules suspended in order that the matter may take its several readings at the present time. If this motion is made in the House of Representatives and there is any opposition, debate is limited to fifteen minutes, no member to occupy more than three minutes.[1] Such a motion can only succeed in extraordinary cases where there is no opposition to the measure.

In either branch a two-thirds vote is necessary to alter anything in the rules, and unanimous consent is required to suspend the rule which requires bills ordered to a third reading to be referred to the Committee on Bills in the Third Reading, or to suspend the rule relative to reconsideration. In the Senate it also takes unanimous consent to suspend the rule requiring engrossed bills to go to the Committee on

[1] House Rule 102.

Engrossed Bills.[1] These rules are a safeguard against hasty legislation.

### ENGROSSMENT OF BILLS

When a measure has been passed through its three stages, or as it is termed, passed to be engrossed, in the second branch, it goes to the office of the Secretary of State to be engrossed on parchment. When so engrossed it is sent to the House, examined by the Committee on Engrossed Bills, and if found to be rightly and truly engrossed, is put upon its final passage. If passed, it is signed by the Speaker, and sent to the Senate, where it goes through the same process,[2] and when passed is signed by the President of that body and laid before the Governor for his approbation. Formerly the process of engrossment on parchment was very slow as the law required bills or resolves to be written out by hand. A few years ago, however, this law was changed so that typewritten engrossment is now legal.

Notice that the bill, after passing to engrossment in the first branch is not engrossed or sent to the Committee on Engrossed Bills in that branch; it must wait before being sent to the Secretary for engrossment until the second branch concurs in passing it to be engrossed. This presumably is to obviate going through the work and expense of writing out measures until they have passed through both branches. Of course the chances are that when measures have been engrossed they will not be defeated. It is rather unusual for them to be even attacked in the enactment stage. Under the rules no amendment to the substance of the bill is in order, and the only amendment allowed is to strike out the enacting clause. This is the opening clause of every bill and reads: "Be it enacted, etc." If that motion carries the bill is of course defeated.

[1] House Rule 103; Senate Rule 63. [2] See Joint Rule 17.

When the measure comes back from the committee on engrossed bills it is wrapped around the original bill and placed in a tin with other engrossed bills on the desk of the presiding officer. He takes them out and announces, "The following engrossed bills reported by the Committee on Engrossed Bills to be rightly and truly engrossed will now be put upon their final passage." If any one wishes to defeat one of these bills now is the time to move to strike out the enacting clause. As a rule all the fighting has taken place at previous stages, and unless something has happened to change the minds of members there is little to be gained by a contest at this stage. But if a contest is to take place, the member interested in making the opposition usually asks the presiding officer to notify him when the matter comes back from the Committee on Engrossed Bills, because measures at that stage are not placed in the calendar, and otherwise they might slip through without being noticed. The presiding officer accordingly sends a page down to notify the member that the matter is going to be read and the member can proceed to contest it at once or may move to have debate on it postponed. The measure, if it goes successfully through this stage, is signed by the Speaker and sent to the Senate, where it goes to the Committee on Engrossed Bills and when reported upon by them after examination and comparison as rightly and truly engrossed it is signed by the President and sent immediately to the Governor.[1]

## Bills and Resolves

When one picks up the Blue Book he reads as the title "Acts and Resolves." Now a resolve rather than a bill may accompany a petition when introduced; like bills they

[1] While an enacted bill may be reconsidered, there is no requirement that it be held for twenty-four hours (see Senate Rule 8 and House Rule 15).

may also be filed on leave or they may be taken from the files of the previous year, if they happen in that year to have been referred to the next General Court.

A "resolve" differs from an "act" in that it is of a temporary nature and does not provide for lasting legislation. It is more like a resolution. Thus it may provide for an appropriation from the treasury of the commonwealth or contain an expression of opinion that money should be appropriated or that certain other things should be done, or it may deal with such matters as the appointment of an investigating committee or the ratification of acts done by a Justice of the Peace or by a Notary after the expiration of his commission. It is sometimes difficult for petitioners to tell the difference and in doubtful cases they should ask the clerk whether the request for legislation should be embodied in a bill or in a resolve. Often, too, committees make the change from one to the other and report in the shape of a resolve something which may have been introduced as a bill or as a bill what may have been erroneously put in as a resolve.

## General and Special Laws

We also find that there are "general" and "special" laws. For the last fifteen or twenty years special laws have been printed every year with the general laws, and have been separately issued triennially. Before that time they were published every five years. The Legislature of 1914, however, made provision that hereafter special as well as general laws should be published yearly, each in a separate volume.

The distinction between a *general* and a *special* law is sometimes hazy and the Secretary's office itself has difficulty in deciding which label a law should bear. In case of doubt the matter is placed in the volume on General Laws. Broadly speaking, legislation affecting the state at large, or counties or districts, may be classed as general laws, likewise all legislation relating to State Boards or Commissions or to courts which touch state or county expenses. Special laws, on the other hand, are laws affecting a city, town, corporation or individual.

### Miscellaneous Points in Procedure

Thus far in the discussion of legislative proceedings several matters of importance that might properly have been taken up were omitted so as not to complicate the direct questions dealt with. For instance, no description has been given as to the method of nominating and electing the presiding officer of each branch; no space has been devoted to the methods of limiting debate; nothing has been said as to how points of order are decided and no attempt has been made to explain what is meant by matters being "finally rejected."

### How Presiding Officers are Chosen

The positions of President of the Senate and Speaker of the House are much sought after. These offices are not only places of power and dignity in themselves but stepping stones to higher political honors. A contest almost invariably takes place, therefore, when a presiding officer resigns or retires. It is very unusual for one to ensue if the old President of the Senate or Speaker of the House is to return. Where the field is left open, however, the candidates announce themselves soon after the session is closed and organize their bands of followers, carrying on a campaign through the summer. Until after the election in November nobody can tell definitely who will be members of the new Legislature, but nevertheless former members, if they should be candidates at the polls, are very apt to be returned again, and if pledges of support can be obtained from them it is a great help not only because of their own votes, but because of the influence they will have with new members. The active candidate for presiding officer will, of course, pledge as many prospective aspirants as he can, whether before or after the primaries, and if he can get a promise from all the candidates of his party at the primaries so much the better. If not, he gets what he can and often will support the ones that favor him against those that do not declare at all or declare themselves against him. As a rule men are not very apt to declare themselves one way or the other even after they are nominated at the primaries, but wait until they are elected at the polls and even then most of them are slow about taking sides. Very often one of the candidates has such an overwhelming lead that the others retire from the contest before the Legislature meets. If they do not retire and the contest is carried to a vote the first test comes in the caucus of the members. These caucuses are called, just before the Legislature meets, by the older members of each branch. The Senators of each political party receive notice to meet at a certain room in the State House and the Representatives of each political party are summoned to meet in another, each to hold a separate caucus for the nomination of President or Speaker and of a clerk and chaplain. These caucuses are held two or three days before the Legislature meets. Here nominating speeches take place and the party candidates are chosen. When the Legislature meets the first business is to organize, and the senior member present takes the chair in each branch until a presiding officer is chosen. The senior member, of course, is not the oldest member in point of age but is the man whose first appearance as a senator or representative antedates that of any of the others. Thus a member who first came to the Senate in 1890 or previously is senior to an older man who first came in 1891.

When this senior member has taken the chair and called the House to order a vote is taken to elect a presiding officer. This is done by passing the ballot box, or, if the members so vote, by calling the roll, and the candidate receiving the highest number of votes is elected to the chair. He then is duly escorted to his seat and makes his address to the assembled members after which a clerk and chaplain are elected. Committees are then announced and notice is sent to the other branch that the body is organized. After the two bodies have elected a Sergeant-at-Arms, notice is sent to the Governor through a joint committee that the whole Legislature is duly organized. As a rule, of course, the Republican members all vote for the nominee of their own caucus and the Democratic members for the nominee of theirs. Every so often, however, party bonds are loosely regarded and, as we saw a few years ago with the rise of the Progressives, caucuses do not necessarily control. Thus, in the election of Mr. Walker as Speaker for a third term, his followers thought it advisable to require a roll-call so they could know how the members voted, and, as they thought, keep their followers more surely in line.

### Absences

In case the presiding officer is to be absent during the session he may appoint a member to take his place. He can only do this, however, for three days at a time. At the end of that period if he has not again designated who should preside, the senior member present takes the chair and presides until a Speaker *pro tempore* or a new Speaker is duly elected; and this matter takes precedence over all other business. In case the presiding officer dies, or resigns, or is away, or in case the member named by him to preside in his absence is not present, again the senior member presides until an election takes place as described above.[1]

There is a rule in both branches of the Legislature that a member shall not be absent more than two days at a time without leave nor shall he stay away without leave at all unless there is a quorum without him.[2] But few of the members know of this rule, and if a member should ask leave of the presiding officer to be away it would be regarded as a joke. However, most members of the Legislature are not there to neglect their duties and the attendance is good.

If members are leaving the session in great numbers or if there is any danger of losing a quorum, the presiding officer can order the doors closed and then of course no member can leave without special permission as the door-keepers will not let him out without the consent of the presiding officer.

## Maintenance of Discipline

The members are usually well-behaved, especially if the presiding officer is a man of power and firmness. Excessive noise from conversation while a member is speaking is usually the chief annoyance. This can generally be stopped by the pounding of the Speaker's gavel or by a verbal reprimand, and it is in the House with its two hundred and forty members rather than in the smaller branch that these measures are apt to be necessary at times. Compared with the noise in the Federal House of Representatives and in some other legislative halls the Massachusetts body is quiet and orderly. In Washington, unless the subject of debate is of unusual importance, few Congressmen make any serious attempt to listen. In some legislative bodies in Continental

[1] See Rules 4 and 5 of the Senate, and 7 and 8 of the House.

[2] Senate Rule 11; House Rule 17.

Europe where the presiding officer is provided with a bell instead of a gavel, pandemonium often reigns.

If a member is insolent, or obstreperous, or breaks any of the rules of the House he may be required to make satisfactory explanation, and until he has done so he is not allowed to vote or to speak except to make his excuses. This has been done where a member used objectionable language about another member in debate and subsequently refused to apologize. In this case a committee was appointed to consider the matter. They reported that until due apology was made the offending member's privileges should be curtailed. It was some time before an apology enabled the offender to be reinstated.

## Where Private Interests are Concerned

There is a rule against members' serving on committees on questions where their private right distinct from the public interest is immediately concerned.[1] A point of order, however, will not lie on the ground that two of the members of the committee reporting the bill were ineligible under this rule.[2] In connection with this rule, another which is germane to the subject should be taken up, namely, the rule that "No member shall vote upon any question where his private right is immediately concerned distinct from the public interest."[3]

These two prohibitions are put together in the Senate under Rule 10, while in the House they are provided for by two separate rules. The rulings of presiding officers on this point are interesting and the distinction drawn between private rights and public interest seems rather broad. For

[1] Senate Rule 10; House Rule 24.

[2] "Notes of Rulings" under House Rule 24.

[3] House Rule 63; under Senate Rule 10.

instance, "in the case of a bill relative to the common use of tracks by two or more street railway companies it was held that it was not a matter in which the private right of the senator, who was President of the street railway company, could be said to be immediately concerned as distinct from the public interest."[1] Under House Rule 63 it has been similarly held that in the case of a creditor or stockholder of the Eastern Railroad, he could vote on a bill "for the relief of the Eastern Railroad Company and the securing of its debts and liabilities, inasmuch as said creditor's or stockholder's interest was not distinct from the public interest but was inseparably mixed with it."

It has also been held that a director of a bank which has petitioned for an increase of capital was "not to be excluded by interest from voting on a motion to instruct the Committee on Banks and Banking to report leave to withdraw on all petitions by banks for an increase of capital." On the other hand, "In the case of a 'bill to equalize the bounties of our soldiers' which provided for paying certain sums of money to a particular class of persons described in the bill," it has been held "that a member who, under the provisions of the bill would be entitled to $200, had such an interest as would deprive him of the right to vote."

"The proper time to raise a point of order questioning the right of a member to vote on account of interest, is after the roll has been called and the member's vote recorded."[2]

## Deciding Points of Order

Of course the most usual point of order to raise against a measure is that the bill is beyond the scope of the petition; but in a hot debate points of order are raised because a

[1] "Notes of Rulings" under Senate Rule 10.

[2] "Notes of Rulings" under House Rule 63 and references there cited.

member is not talking to the question, or is using unparliamentary language, or for all sorts of reasons. In the great majority of cases the question will not be a difficult one and a ruling can be given by the presiding officer off-hand. Sometimes, too, advance information is given that a point of order may be raised. In this case the presiding officer and clerk have an opportunity to look into it. In close and important cases, however, it is necessary for the chair to take the matter under advisement. In such cases the matter is usually postponed without question to enable the presiding officer to look into the point of order. I remember with great distinctness one point of order that was raised during my Speakership, because the matter was of very far-reaching importance. During the contest over a measure to change the site of the Registry of Deeds of Plymouth County from the town of Plymouth to the city of Brockton, a point of order was raised that the bill reported by the committee was beyond the scope of the petition. I had heard rumors that a point of order might be raised, but had not looked into the matter as I thought the question would probably be fought out on its merits, since, if the bill were thrown out on a mere point of order that would probably be an additional incentive to continue the fight another year, whereas if the bill was decisively defeated or went through, the whole question would be finally disposed of. However, the point cf order was made by one of the members who favored leaving the Registry where it was, and I took the matter under advisement. After consultations with the Clerk of the Senate as well as with the Clerk of the House, the matter being of such great importance, I reached the conclusion that the bill was beyond the scope of the petition and ruled accordingly. Strange to say, instead of stirring up animosity or providing any greater incentive to push the measure another year, the whole proposal seems to have dropped out of sight. Although a ruling by the chair is not necessarily final, as a member can appeal from it, no appeal is in order unless seconded and even when seconded the members will always vote to sustain a ruling unless it is manifestly unfair. Consequently an appeal is seldom taken.

## Discouraging Special Acts

There is a rule[1] providing that "When the object of an application can be secured without a special act under existing laws, or without detriment to the public interests, by a general law, the committee to which the matter is referred shall report such general law, or leave to withdraw, or ought not to pass, as the case may be." This is an excellent rule, and instead of being merely in the rules of the Legislature it is embodied in the constitutions of some of the western states.

If it is not desired to observe the principles embodied in this provision, it is of little more use to put it in a constitution than to have it in the rules of the Legislature. But the principle is absolutely right and fair, because if any privileges are to be issued they should be given broadly to all in any line of business and not meted out to favorites.

## Final Rejections

In an earlier part of this chapter, reference was made to a possible distinction between matters going from one branch to the other where in one case a motion to substitute and a contest had been made in the first branch, and where in the other case the committees' report had been accepted without contest.[2] In the first case if the second branch substitutes the measure and it comes back to the first branch, it is

[1] House Rule 30; Senate Rule 16. [2] See *above*, p. 110, and note 1.

thrown out under the rules as it had been finally rejected there. In the second case it could come back or another measure substantially the same could be acted on, because the matter had not been finally rejected.[1]

Rule 49 of the House provides, "When a bill, order, petition, memorial or remonstrance has been finally rejected by the House, no measure substantially the same shall be introduced by any committee or member during the same session."

There have been numerous rulings on this point both in the Senate and in the House. They show that the rule expresses a general principle of parliamentary law. It has been held that the fact that a bill has been finally rejected in one branch does not prevent its introduction in another; but where a bill or measure has been rejected by both branches this rule, as well as parliamentary practice, would prevent another measure substantially the same from being introduced in either branch at that session. Even if one branch has passed such a measure, courtesy between the two will not prevent the second branch from laying the matter aside. "The rejection of a measure does not prevent the consideration of a measure substantially the same if it was introduced previously to such rejection."

It will be noticed in the House rule that the words used are "finally rejected by the House," whereas the Senate rule reads "finally rejected." Thus it has been held in rulings by Speakers of the House that "a bill passed to be engrossed by the House but rejected by the Senate is not by this rule barred from being again introduced in the House."

A bill is regarded as not substantially the same if it has been changed in any essential particular; thus it has been held that "the rejection of a bill providing for permanent

[1] Notes of Rulings on House 49, and also those on Senate Rule 54.

clerical assistance does not exclude the subsequent introduction of a resolve providing for temporary clerical assistance." It has also been held that after a bill was rejected one of the sections of the bill could be introduced without violation of the rule.

Reference to the next General Court seems to be not a final rejection and where a bill has been read a third time it is held too late to raise the point of order that it was substantially the same as a bill already rejected, and thus improperly before the House.[1]

This last ruling is consistent with the decisions under House Rule 30 where it has been held that a violation of that rule cannot be raised after a bill has been ordered to a third reading and with those under Rule 47, where it has been held that substitution of a bill for the report of a committee makes it too late to raise the point of order that the bill is broader in its scope than when it was offered to the Committee.[2] Massachusetts has a liberal Constitution as I have shown. The rules of her Legislature are liberal too. There are only four other State Legislatures, according to Mr. Reinsch, that require a report from a committee within a certain time. In Massachusetts every committee has to report on all measures sent to it. There is no stifling of matters in committee. Hearings are given, and generously advertised, on all subjects, whether of great or little importance. Professor Reinsch says:

> . . . the General Court of Massachusetts is in all respects nearest the people, and most responsive of any American legislature to intelligent public opinion.[3] . . . It is indeed quite necessary that all states should adopt and enforce legislation like that of Massachusetts, which requires sufficient notice of all committee meetings.[4]

[1] Notes of Rulings on House Rule 49.

[2] See *above*, p. 91.

[3] *American Legislatures and Legislative Methods*, p. 174. [4] *Ibid.*, p. 257.

# INDEX

# INDEX

Bei Fragen zur Produktsicherheit wenden Sie sich bitte an:
If you have any questions regarding product safety,
please contact:

Walter de Gruyter GmbH
Genthiner Straße 13
10785 Berlin
productsafety@degruyterbrill.com